Gail

Always & Always

[signature]

6-16-86

PAUL J. FRIDAY, Ph.D

FRIDAY'S LAWS

How to Become Normal When You're Not And How To Stay Normal When You Are

From
Bradley Oak Publications

**Successful Living
Requires Effective Thinking;
To Know A Little Quicker When Our
Crazy Ideas Are Crazy**

*I'm Normal;
Why Aren't Other People Like Me?*

Library of Congress Cataloging in Publication Data

International Standard Book Number: 0-9669938-0-2

Library of Congress Catalog Card Number: 98-83282

I have used fictitious names throughout this book. These names have no relationship between characters described in this book and any patients or acquaintances that I have known in either my professional or personal life.

Printed by Geyer Printing, Pittsburgh, PA

Manufactured in the United States of America

Published by
Bradley Oak Publications
P.O. Box 111595
1310 Old Freeport Road
Pittsburgh, Pennsylvania 15238
SAN: 299 – 8238

THE WORLD WE HAVE CREATED

IS A PRODUCT OF OUR THINKING;

IT CANNOT BE CHANGED WITHOUT

CHANGING OUR THINKING.

- Albert Einstein

This book is dedicated to

Clarence E. Giese

My Mentor
and
My Friend

WHAT OTHERS ARE SAYING ABOUT FRIDAY'S LAWS

M.Scott Peck redefined psychotherapy as *The Road Less Traveled*. Paul J. Friday's eight laws of effective thinking provide the guide posts that allow the trip to take place. A clever and insightful description of what makes people change and how they do it.

> David Servan-Schreiber, M.D., Ph.D., Chief of Psychiatry
> University of Pittsburgh Medical Center-Shadyside
> Pittsburgh, Pennsylvania

Friday's Laws is filled with wisdom and humor. It's thought-provoking and innovative. As we all head toward the new millennium, Friday's Laws is a guide to the one thing we all need in our lives—balance. It's totally readable. Paul Friday is among my favorite interviewees. It's like talking to a very caring, very knowledgeable friend. *Friday's Laws* is like that too.

> Patrice King-Brown
> KDKA – TV News, CBS
> Pittsburgh, Pennsylvania

Dr. Paul Friday has helped thousands to understand and manage their feelings of distress. His simple *laws* contain profound truth. This timely book allows a wide audience to benefit from his insights.

> Fred Rubin, M.D., Chairman, Department of Medicine
> University of Pittsburgh Medical Center – Shadyside
> Pittsburgh, Pennsylvania

The Firesign Theater said, 'We're All Bozos On This Bus.' *Friday's Laws* explains why. Friday gets under the hood and explains the mechanics—not of the bus, but of us bozos. When you finish this book, you might still be unclear about why your amygdala is always jumping in ahead of your cerebral cortex, but you'll have a better handle on why everyone is a little crazy. Nuttiness, in moderation, is a survival skill.

> Brian O'Neill, Columnist, Pittsburgh Post-Gazette
> Pittsburgh, Pennsylvania

Dr. Friday has done an amazing job of presenting Cognitive Behavioral Therapy in an exciting manner which anyone can read and enjoy. Simultaneously humorous and serious, Dr. Friday distills the essence of the well studied and highly effective field of CBT. *Friday's Laws* speaks to crazy ideas of worthlessness and hopelessness and how to turn these ideas into healthier ones of hope and optimism. *Friday's Laws* is good reading for all of us still angry that we have to change ourselves, not the rest of the world, if we are to be happy and successful. Through his humor, he helps us to swallow that bitter pill and emerge the better for it.

> Lewis Mehl-Madrona, M.D. , Div. Psychiatry
> University of Pittsburgh Medical Center -Shadyside
> Medical Director, Center for Complimentary Medicine
> Pittsburgh, Pennsylvania
> Author, *Coyote Medicine*

Dr. Friday's book will reward you with a permanent record of his intellectual arguments and patient stories with an emotionally uplifting dialogue. I have found it to be the most relevant and practical psychology book that I have read.

> Jeffrey B. Riley
> Past President, AmSECT
> San Clemente, California

Dr. Paul Friday has instilled an enormous experience into a well organized approach to thoughts and human actions/reactions. In contrast to many treatises on the subject, this book is easy to understand. It is a delight to read, and incredibly meaningful for its impact on our everyday lives.

W. Gerald Rainer, M.D., Clinical Prof. of Surgery
University of Colorado Health Sciences Center
Denver, Colorado

For everyone who has ever wondered about what constitutes normal and how to get there, *Friday's Laws* provides a map plus written directions to help you on your way. Clever, engaging, and eminently readable; mental mysteries are solved and the layers of the human psyche are peeled away much like an onion to reveal the reasons that you act, react, and even think the way that you do. Dr. Friday defines reality — and your perception of it — with eight undeniable truths. His take on the human journey from "womb-to-tomb" is a great ride that engages the reader from start to finish.

Alicia Maloney, Producer, AgeWise
UPMC HealthNews – PBS-TV
Pittsburgh, Pennsylvania

Friday's Laws are universally applicable to everyday life. As a neuroscientist I particularly enjoyed his ability to correlate the limbic system to the neocortex and how that relationship psychologically manifests itself. I am sure his readers will find this a useful and enlightening book.

David S. Zorub, M.D., VP, Clinical Affairs
Chair, Dept. Surgery, UPMC-Shadyside
Chairman of the Board,
Allegheny County Medical Society
Pittsburgh, Pennsylvania

Paul Friday is right, 'Life is Difficult', but by following his re-markably simple laws, mine has become easier and more satisfy-ing. You have nothing to lose and everything to gain by reading this book.

Nancy Polinsky-Johnson, Writer, Producer
Pittsburgh, Pennsylvania

Paul Friday challenges his own 1st Law—Life Is Difficult, with brain strategies to help you think with efficiency, and act with wisdom.

Ann Devlin, Broadcast Journalist
PBS-TV
Pittsburgh, Pennsylvania

Honest and understandable, an essential read. In this stunning new book, Dr. Friday suggests ways we all can use to reach a higher level of understanding ourselves. Filled with information and tips to improve human relationships, you don't read a page of this book without the feeling that you have a deeper understand-ing of who you are, and how you think. I was moved with its wonderful surprises and new insights into what is normal and what is not. Dr. Friday teaches valuable lessons; *Friday's Laws* can transform your life.

Eleanor Schano, Broadcast Journalist
AgeWise – PBS-TV
Pittsburgh, Pennsylvania

TABLE OF CONTENTS

Forward

The Declaration of Independence of the United States of America proclaims that the right to pursue happiness is inalienable: along with life and liberty. Although most people believe they would be happier if they had more money, wealth only increases short-term happiness and has little, if any, effect on long-term well-being. As Dr. Paul Friday details in *Friday's Laws*, happiness comes from a proper attitude or perspective; not from wealth alone.

In *Friday's Laws* psychologist Paul Friday presents eight succinct principles to help readers become normal when they are not, or to stay normal despite the stresses of their lives.

Friday's first law is that *life is difficult*. Everyday people are confronted with very real challenges such as chronic stressors or serious life events. There is no escaping the human condition. Indeed, the first Noble Truth of the Compassionate Buddha is that "life entails hardship."

The nature of these stressors can be readily identified by all readers and are often reflected in the examples given in this book. Cars break down; trains run late; bosses are sometimes unreasonable; and appliances do not always work. Even worse, however, is the fact that loved ones get sick and die; cherished relationships fail; and friends disappoint us.

Nonetheless, the burdens can be made tolerable and our lives can be made enjoyable for those who are able to keep the right perspectives. The other laws of Paul Friday explain how we can survive and even prosper in a difficult world. The harsh events and daily stressors can be made more palatable if we focus on controlling what we know we can control: our attitudes or beliefs about these events.

As a clinical psychologist, Dr. Friday has treated thousands of patients with a wide range of problems. Through listening to his patients, he has identified the common threads which occur in their concerns. As a well-respected public speaker, Dr. Friday is adept at explaining psychological concepts in a clear manner with relevant illustrations and examples.

Friday's Laws contains the core principles that Dr. Friday has espoused over the years. It avoids professional jargon and presents clear principles intermixed with concrete examples. It is a useful book with information on the beliefs or attitudes that can lessen the impact of harmful life events and chronic stressors.

Read. Study. Enjoy.

    Dr. Samuel Knapp
    Professional Affairs Officer
    Pennsylvania Psychological Association

Preface

This is a book about how to become normal when
you're not,
How to stay normal when you are,
and how to separate the two when the need arises.

Human beings are interested in other human beings. We like to know how others live, what they feel, how they cope and survive on their womb-to-tomb trips. What other human beings do to *win* at living becomes an informational target for us. We emulate behaviors that we feel are potentially good and productive; we avoid the behaviors that are potentially bad and non-productive.

Friday's Laws is based on my work with thousands of patients in well over 50,000 hours of a clinical practice. Hundreds of lectures, radio shows, and television interviews propelled the creation of this work. This book will show you how both normal and not-so-normal people exist side by side in this difficult world. By emulating the thinking and behaviors of *normal* people, it is hoped that your life will improve in *quality* regardless of the *quantity* of living that remains for you.

We all struggle to carry the baggage of our own lives. An elderly physician who worked most of his life with dying patients, helping to make their end-of-life stage more comfortable, gave me an insightful perspective. He told me he had never met nor worked with anybody, especially at the end of his or her life, who had an empty plate. Getting to a point where we have done all, and have nothing left to do, is not the goal of effective thinking or living. ***The goal of effective living is to think effectively; to know when we have crazy ideas.***

My goal with this book is to take you on an interesting trip. I want to take you on a journey into the human mind—a sojourn that will help you to become normal if you are not, to stay normal if you are, and to know how to separate the two when the need arises.

Introduction

FRIDAY'S LAWS

How To Become Normal When You're Not And
How To Stay Normal When You Are

Normal people have crazy ideas.
Crazy people have crazy ideas.
Normal people know a little quicker when their crazy ideas are crazy.
Crazy people are convinced that their crazy ideas are normal.

The psyche of *every* human who has ever lived has probed the essence of these four sentences. Throughout the history of man's existence here on earth, every man and woman, and most children, have questioned what "normal" and what "crazy" are. Humans, at various times throughout their lives, have questioned their sanity. The questioning of what is normal and what is not happens not just once or twice but occurs in each of us many times throughout our lives. Millionaires and paupers alike question their normalcy; the learned and the ignorant; the powerful and the meek.

A universal response to the question of whether you are normal or whether you are crazy is to say, with little reflection: I'm OK. It is the other people who have a problem.

All humans, including you, have questioned whether they are *normal*. All humans have also questioned what it takes to be normal, and how far away they actually are from being *crazy*.

You are about to discover what it takes to *think normally* and what you can do when you have *crazy* ideas. The key to this discovery is going to be an understanding of how the human brain works.

How Does Your Brain Work?

Mankind's knowledge of brain function changed radically on the afternoon of September 13, 1848. A 25-year-old, mild mannered, working foreman for a Vermont railroad company was using a 13- pound tamping rod to prepare a blasting charge for a new rail line. A spark was created when the iron rod struck a rock in a pre-drilled hole. Unfortunately, the hole had already been charged with gunpowder. Instantly, the world had the tragic event it needed to restructure its concept of human brain function. The first recorded (self-inflicted) pre-frontal lobotomy was performed. This three-and-a-half-foot iron rod was propelled up and through Mr. Phineas Gage's skull and brain. It passed behind his left eye, separating his left frontal lobe from the rest of his cerebral cortex. The tamping rod landed about 30 meters away from its original launching site, still coated with the residue of Phineas' bone, brain, and hair. Astonishingly, Phineas not only survived the acute phase of the accident but lived an additional 15 years. (Good downward drainage and amazing antiseptic techniques [for the time] by Phineas' physicians, Drs. Williams and J. M. Harlow, are credited for his medical recovery.)

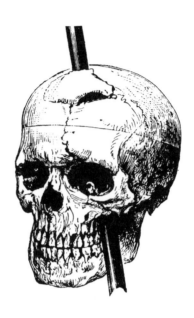

Phineas P. Gage's skull, depicted with the 3-foot 7-inch-long, 13-pound, inch and a quarter diameter tamping iron in situ. Harlow, J.M., 1868. Recovery from the Passage of an Iron Bar through the Head. Publications of the Massachusetts Medical Society, 2, 327 – 347.

Prior to this event, the frontal portion of the brain was basically considered to be irrelevant in human functioning. However, Phineas P. Gage was never the same. He was no longer fit company among women and innocents. Swearing, cursing, ranting, and raving were now the hallmarks of this previously gentle man. The ventral, or front section, of the frontal lobe was to be evermore regarded as the storage site for control and values. From 1860 onward, mankind's knowledge of the relationship between brain function and personality changed radically.

The terrible accident that happened to Mr. Gage one and a half centuries ago was an important event for all of us. It is a key to our understanding of when we are *thinking effectively* and when we are having *crazy ideas*.

The Stir Crazy Sign

As a clinical psychologist, I work with a variety of patients, many of whom have a wide spectrum of emotional problems. Several years ago, I was talking with a particularly distressed patient. It was about a month prior to a lecture that I was scheduled to give in Texas. My patient did something that gave me a wonderful understanding and insight into how humans communicate, and how the human brain works.

Robert had been a patient of mine for some time, and I was quite concerned for his long-term well-being. Although we had discussed his suicidal ideation's, as the psychiatric community is wont to call them, I was equally concerned with the *crazy ideas* that he kept silently, and sometimes not so silently, repeating to himself. Over and over again Robert would relate these anxiety provoking ideas of worthlessness and hopelessness. *Where* these ideas come from is the fodder of psychoanalytic struggles. But, as a cognitive therapist, I was much more concerned with understanding and helping Robert to substitute *healthier* ideas of realistic hope and perhaps to offer a degree of optimism to what had been months of wandering in a desert of fitful despair. Then he did it. As he said, *"I sometimes think I'm crazy,"* he made a slight hand gesture. A very small hand movement that was done very rapidly. It was as if a bomblet had exploded in my own brain.

"Robert, what did you just do there?"
"Where?" he asked.
"There. With your hand. What did you just do?" I asked.
"What? This?" he said. *As he moved his hand he repeated,*
"I sometimes think I'm crazy."

More fireworks. What a beautifully simplistic hand gesture. In all the hours that I'd invested in the human struggles of psychotherapy, I had never connected basic brain function with common psycho-pathologies as well as Robert had done on that afternoon.

In order to test this growing concept, I asked my next ten patients the same question.

What hand gesture do you use to indicate that someone is *crazy* ?

All ten people, without exception, did the same hand gesture that Robert had done. How curiously simplistic. I decided to try a larger group, so I posed the question to a number of physician colleagues during a Medical Grand Rounds. In unison, they all did the same gesture that Robert had done a week earlier. How could so many different people, with such diversified backgrounds, use the same gesture to indicate that someone was perceived as being mentally unbalanced? So let's take a chance and try this on a really large group, I thought.

I was preparing to give a talk at an international medical congress held in Dallas, Texas. The group was to be addressed on the emotional stress that medical professionals experience in operating rooms.

I approached the podium in Dallas and looked out over a sea of almost 2,000 faces. Thoracic surgeons, perfusionists, operating room nurses, and nurse anesthetists, literally from around the world, had gathered for an annual meeting to discuss the latest technical advances in cardiac bypass surgery and its related disciplines. They were born and lived in large cities and small villages. Diverse cultures, religions, and beliefs were represented. The average age of the audience was probably thirty-five to forty, and there were a few more males than females present. What a beautiful cross-sectional representation of the world sat in front of me.

"I don't want you to do anything until I say the word *now*," I began.

"Think back to when you were children. Perhaps you were on a school playground, or sitting with a group of your friends at a nearby store. Someone, perhaps a teacher, an ostracized peer, or even a stranger walked nearby. He or she was within hearing distance from you and your friends, and you wanted to indicate to your friends that the person was *crazy* without them hearing you. What hand gesture would you use to show your friends that you thought this person was *crazy*?

"Please do not make the gesture yet," I continued. "Just think about it for a second."

"Those of you in the front of the auditorium, please stand up and turn around so you can face your colleagues at the back of the room. Those in the middle, please look to your colleagues on either side." Giggling began as a slow nervous rumbling as this huge group began to twist in different directions. "Again, when I say the word *now*, I'd like you to make a hand movement that you would use to indicate that you thought someone was *crazy*."

"*Now*," I said.

At that moment, 2000 people made the same hand gesture that you are now doing and the term "*The Stir Crazy Sign*" was created.

A slow rotation of the index finger back and forth or around and around, at the side of the head, is *The Stir Crazy Sign*.

What had been giggling now erupted into uproarious laughter. This was such a simple, universal gesture for stating non-verbally that someone was considered *crazy*. When the group calmed down, a description of what began to be called *"The Stir Crazy Sign"* ensued.

When the ventral section of the frontal lobe[1] (the storage site for human values) is *in opposition* with the temporal lobe (the area of the brain responsible for storing the primitive, emotional sense of self and survival), *while excluding* the cerebral cortex (where language and logic is located), humans are said to be *crazy*.

It may be an over-simplification, but *when values and emotions clash, and the logical, problem-solving section of the brain is excluded from the thought process, humans experience various degrees of anxiety and depression.* When we go back and forth between our values (should/should not, must/must not) and our emotions, we begin to feel uncomfortable sensations. When this conflict is pushed to an extreme, humans can be said to go crazy.

Imagine the reaction of a child when an authority figure screams at him or her. I remember being at a local mall and watching an exhausted mother scream and berate her four-year-old child. "You have to move faster or we'll miss the bus!" The child, also exhausted, screamed even louder in her weary defiance. A struggle of wills ensued with neither the mother nor daughter winning the conflict. The bus came and went; the mutual struggling continued, another bus came along, and, finally, the combatants departed.

This happens inside our brains when *The Stir Crazy Sign* is at play. When our values (should, have to, got to, better, and must) and emotions (tired, scared, don't want to) are in opposition, we can begin to feel inside, and behave outside, like that mother and child at the mall. We experience this conflict when we fail to refer to the problem-solving part of the brain, also the station of language and logic.

The Other Side of *Stir Crazy*

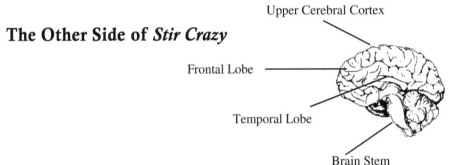

For months after the Dallas lecture, I mentally expanded that insightful session with my patient, Robert, and the confirmation of thousands of people that *The Stir Crazy Sign* was a universal hand gesture for being unstable or going *crazy*.

What if, instead of opposition, there was *agreement* among the various areas of the cerebral cortex? What do we have when the forward section of the frontal lobe and the deeper temporal lobe are in agreement, while there is still exclusion of the upper area of the cerebral cortex?

What do we call a positive synthesis of values and emotions, while still having exclusion of logic and reason? These are **Beliefs**. When humans believe in something, be it a belief that something

is or is not going to happen, that something has or has not occurred, is or is not so, then we can say that their values and
emotions are in sync. The logic and reason functions of the brain
are not being utilized as much as the other two sections of the
brain that encompass emotions and values. We may want to give
logical proofs (rationalizations) of these things, but the basis for
these beliefs remains the agreement between values and emotions
as the underpinning of the rationalization.

Just as increasing **conflict** between brain sections causes
increasing degrees of anxiety and depression, then we must also
note varying degrees of **agreement** between sections of the brain.
Agreement or mutual support between the ventral area of the
frontal lobe and the temporal lobe (thereby increasing exclusion of
the logic/reason section of the brain called the cerebral cortex) can
create as many emotional problems as brain-sectional *conflict*.

When there is a stronger connection between these two brain
sections, the **BELIEF** becomes a **TRUTH**. Even stronger, tighter
connections between the ventral section of the frontal lobe and the
temporal lobe push truths to a deeper, stronger level which we call
FAITH. When faith is extended, and further excludes logic and
reason, we approach **FUNDAMENTALISM**.

If the communicating process between these two brain sections
continues to strengthen and the upper cerebral cortex continues to
be relegated to an ever-diminishing role, our brains lose a sense of
well-rounded balance and we get truly enmeshed in *The Stir Crazy
Sign*.

The next strata of this mysterious world of self-destruction and
the destruction of others excludes and rejects the problem-solving
characteristics of language and logic. Psychopathology emerges
in the form of **TERRORISM**. Picture yourself approaching some

people who are loading the trunk of a car with explosives which they intend to detonate outside of a nearby embassy, palace, or place of worship. The terrorists are about to set the charge. Imagine the response to the suggestion that they discuss the conflict that they are having with the particular institution or group they are about to destroy. The chances of successfully using logic with an extremist, regardless of the terrorist's goal or ideal, for the purpose of discussing or dissuading an action, are not good.

Perhaps the ultimate connection of these two brain sections, to the **total exclusion** of logic and reason, is **MASS SUICIDE**. In the mid-1990s, members of the American cult *Heaven's Gate*, who donned their black tennis shoes for a trip to the far side of the Hale-Bopp comet, had *total exclusion* of logic and reason. These poor souls so welded their pre-frontal and temporal lobes together, and had such repulsion of their upper cerebral cortex, that reason became unreasonable, and self-destruction became a viable alternative to existence. The world discovered with fascinated horror, a mass suicide.

On one side of *The Stir Crazy Sign* coin, the opposition of brain sections makes one seem crazy. The other side of this coin, the agreement and fusion of brain sections, can be illustrated by this ladder, progressing in the intensity of *craziness.*

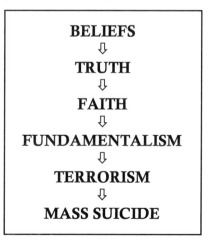

BELIEFS
⇩
TRUTH
⇩
FAITH
⇩
FUNDAMENTALISM
⇩
TERRORISM
⇩
MASS SUICIDE

Friday's Laws is intended as a guide to how to maintain a balance between the major sections of the brain, thus avoiding *Stir Craziness*. A **balance** of **values**, **emotions**, and **logical** thinking is what I call *Thinking Effectively*.

The laws in *Friday's Laws* are more like laws of nature than man-made laws. Man-made laws are formed to help direct and/or control human behaviors. Speed limits and religious command-ments are examples of these laws. Laws of nature, like *Friday's Laws*, contain no directives like *you should*, or *you have to*. This book describes the human condition in *balance*. It is not a directive for human behavior.

An aspiration of this book is to help people live more effective lives by knowing a little quicker when their crazy ideas are crazy. A theoretical goal is to help balance the bio-electrical activity that flows among the ventral area of the frontal lobe, the temporal lobe, and the upper cerebral cortex. With a balance in brain function, living can be more effective, successful, and enjoyable.

Friday's Laws, which create the framework of this book, de-scribe the human circumstance when it works right. They are laws driven by the upper cerebral cortex. These laws are not driven by the forward section of the frontal lobe, where learned values are stored and retrieved. Nor do they originate in the temporal lobe, where deep-seated, survival emotions are hoarded.

Friday's Laws are eight mediating concepts that will help maintain emotional or mental balance by short-circuiting the **domination** of either values or emotions. *Values and emotions are, of course, critical components to healthy thinking and effective living.* But the risk of *The Stir Crazy Sign* bullies every human on a daily basis. Recognizing these *crazy thoughts* a little quicker will help you be as psychologically successful as possible.

People who think effectively know that:

1. Life is difficult.
2. Perception is reality.
3. Change is the toughest thing a human being can do.
4. You can never change another human being; you can only change yourself. Once you change, they change, but you can not change them.
5. I am responsible for everything I do and say. I am not responsible for your response.
6. The future and the past are seldom as good or as bad as we anticipate or remember.
7. Nobody has a squeaky-clean psyche.
8. The only thing that lasts forever is . . . NOW.

A Caveat

Therapeutic resolution for serious emotional problems is *not* the purpose of this book. Hopefully, you *will* understand much better what the human condition is like when it works effectively.

As the Epilogue will discuss, resolving deep emotional problems is not an easy endeavor and takes a great deal more than reading a book to be accomplished. These *Laws* do not, as Susan, a cancer patient of mine, pointed out, permit despair, allow a frantic, panic disordered patient to become calm. Nor will they help a dying patient find peace. That is not the purpose of *Friday's Laws*. H.L.Mencken was quoted by President Jimmy Carter as saying, "For every human problem, there is a solution that is simple, neat, and *wrong*."

If, however, you are living on a basically stable emotional platform, then reading this book will be an enjoyable journey for you. Think of it as a healthy guide for keeping the burdens and difficulties of life from overwhelming you in your daily struggles

defining you as a unique person on this earth. May your journey
be an insightful one. I believe this book will help you discover
how to

Think Effectively.
Know When You Have a Crazy Idea.

Please enjoy.

FRIDAY'S LAWS

1. **Life Is Difficult.**

2. Perception Is Reality.

3. Change Is The Toughest Thing A Human Being Can Do.

4. You Can Never Change Another Human Being; You Can Only Change Yourself. When You Change, They Change, But You Can Not Change Them.

5. I Am Responsible For Everything I Do And Say. I Am Not Responsible For Your Response.

6. The Future And The Past Are Seldom As Good Or As Bad As We Anticipate Or Remember.

7. No One Has A Squeaky Clean Psyche.

8. The Only Thing That Lasts Forever Is . . . NOW.

1

Life is Difficult.

But why is life difficult ?

It is better to know some of the questions than all of the answers.

James Thurber

For 20 years patients have asked, and I have wondered, what it takes to be *normal*. All of the testing, all of the gentle nudging and forceful budging, and all of the medications lead nowhere as long as this fundamental question, **"What is Normal?"** is not answered.

I spent my initial years of helping people as a therapist turning the questions patients asked back toward them. The proverbial statement, "answer a question with a question," remains a primary approach for many psychotherapists. Someone may invest his or her scarce time, honest effort, and hard-earned money into self-change, but I can't help him or her achieve desired changes unless he or she can answer— *"What do you want to happen? Where do you want to go?"*

As my professional years as a therapist began accumulating, I felt increasingly uneasy in the fundamental shifting of responsibility toward the patient in answering this, the most essential of all therapy questions,

What *is* normal?

I recall taking my third post-graduate course in administering and scoring Rorschach (ink blot) tests. It was during this course that I realized that the *pathology-oriented medical model* was deeply embedded in my field also. The instructor, in over 100 hours of talking about the ten different Rorschach cards, had neglected to describe what a *normal* Rorschach protocol looked like. It was as if no one were allowed to be *normal*. There was little or no discussion of what a test result would include to classify a patient as being *OK*. Although I finally wrestled an answer from the Rorschach expert on what acceptably normal test results would include, I could tell that there was an edge of agitation in his response. I had made him take time away from his unending description of psycho-pathology.

So what is normal?

Normal is thinking effectively.
Knowing when you have a crazy idea.

With the advent of quicker and more efficient approaches to psychotherapy, I began to develop some guidelines for **effective thinking**. Using the previously described model of *The Stir Crazy Sign*, I began the search for upper cerebral cortex guidance (where language and logic are located) to stop the cyclical battles between the ventral section of the frontal lobe (where learned values are stored) and the temporal lobe (where deep-seated survival emotions are generated). A psychology professor might pose, "What principles could the superior cortex utilize so that it could mediate the imbalance and conflicts that are generated out of the frontal lobe and temporal lobe interactions?" As described in the introduction, this bonding and agitation between these two brain sections constitute human *crazy ideas*.

Let me begin with a story about memory as told to me by my wife's Uncle Wilbur.

It seems that there were these three men, a physician, a lawyer, and a psychologist, who were bragging to each other about their high recall and memory functions.

"My memory is so good, claimed the physician, that I can remember my mother changing my diaper."

"That's nothing," declared the lawyer with a certain degree of superior indignation. "My memory is so good, I've just hired a colleague to represent me. You see, I distinctly remember on the day I was born, my mother's obstetrician slapping me. I'm suing him for assault and battery."

"Well, declared the psychologist. My memory is so good, I can remember going to a dance with my father and coming home with my mother."

Date of Conception

Prior to the moment when you were conceived, you had perceptual non-existence. For the eons prior to the date of your conception there was no sensation, no time, and no space. Perhaps we were all in a true fourth, fifth, or sixth dimension?

There was no black, no white, and no gray.
There was no solid, liquid, nor gas.
There was nothingness.

On the momentous day of your conception, at that spectacular moment, one of the millions of sperm in your father's ejaculate burrowed itself through natures' protective lining, deep into the one egg that your mother's ovaries released during that particular, 28 day cycle, and

Your body began to be.

Calculating Your Date of Conception (DC)

When were you conceived? To determine this date, complete the appropriate sections of Table I.

(Scoring hint: When entering the month, use words   and not numbers. For example, write in the word *June***, not the number** *6***.)**

TABLE I

Calculation of **DATES OF CONCEPTION (DC)**for Birth Dates Falling Between **January** and **September**

	MONTH	DATE	YEAR
My birth date is			
Add 3 months			
Subtract 1 year			
Date of conception (DC) was			

Calculation of **DATES OF CONCEPTION (DC)** for Birth Dates Falling Between **October** and **December**

	MONTH	DATE	YEAR
My birth date is			
Add 3 months			
Date of conception (DC) was			

Period of Awe

Why did you let me be born? Why couldn't I have stayed in the deep waters of the womb, rocked to sleep in the dark?
Stephen Mitchell; The Book of Job

The next eight to nine weeks of your existence were explosive in their intensity and wonderment. However, these first two months are not the point of discussion for this book. Approximately two months after your conception, an initiation of *Conditioned Wonder* began. This is called the Period of Awe and can be calculated by completing Table II.

Calculating Your Period of Awe (PA)

When did your temporal lobe, the heart and soul of your brain, begin to be formed? To determine the onset of your Period of Awe (PA), complete the appropriate sections of Table II.

(Scoring hint: When entering the month, write in the word, not the number. For example write the word *June*, not the number 6)

TABLE II

Calculation of **PERIOD OF AWE (PA)** for Dates of Conception (**DC**) Falling Between **January** and **October**

	MONTH	DATE	YEAR
My date of conception (DC) was			
Add 2 months			
Period of awe (PA) began on			

Calculation of **PERIOD OF AWE (PA)** for Dates of Conception (**DC**) Falling In **November or December**

	MONTH	DATE	YEAR
My date of conception (DC) was			
Add 2 months			
Add 1 year			
My period of awe (PA) began on			

Your *Period of Awe* occurred in the span of time from approximately 60 days after your date of conception through the date of your birth. It lasted roughly seven months and is the reason why your life, and the life of every human being who ever has lived, and ever will live, was, is, and will always be . . . ***difficult.***

Sometime between the eighth and ninth week of your gestation (give or take several days) you had an ever-awakening sense of true, non-verbal, existential **Awe**. It was sometime between the eighth and ninth week of your gestation that a microscopic cluster of packed neurons began to develop deep in your temporal lobe. Called the amygdala[2] (Appendix I), this central part of the temporal lobe in your brain began to develop at this time. Its development permitted you to begin to perceive a true state of Awe. You experienced, from the absolute nothingness of nothing, a virtual, instantaneous metamorphosis into *perfection*. For each day of the next seven months, your life became better and more intense in this perfection.

Imagine, with nothing to compare it to, you grew in this perfect state of equilibrium and instant, perpetual homeostasis. You had **no sense of wants, no sense of deeper needs**. You did have **total dependency, vulnerability, and intimacy** (three pivotal constructs which will be discussed in Chapter 7 when *internal success* and *external success* are explored in depth).

During your Period of Awe, you were in heaven with your Maker, an imprinted experience which will instinctively remain with you, as a driving force, for as long as you live.

Every known civilization has developed concepts of a god or gods. Many civilizations have created concepts of a richly envisioned life after death. When the rituals and icon-personalities of formal religions are stripped away, most faiths create a mental and emotional image of a temporal/transcending space. All languages have some translation of the English word *heaven*. These *After-Lives* have pre-birth foundations in conditioned experience. All *heavens* have been experienced pre-linguistically in our temporal lobes. Located above the upper brain stem and below the cerebral cortex, this area, where heaven swirls, incubates the last 28 weeks of our gestation; however, our birth may euphemistically be referred to as the ultimate *ejection-rejection*.

Nature can be cruel, though. Due to a genetic malformation, exposure to a toxin, or an expectant mother's addiction to alcohol or drugs, some humans spend their Period of Awe on a rung of Dante's *Inferno*. The brains and bodies of these poor souls never have a chance to develop in a normal set of conditions. What is left is a tragic potential that is never realized. What would have been a difficult life becomes torturous if there is sufficient consciousness to recognize the loss. If not, the individual's life becomes a test of the loving parents, whose adaptation to the raising of an exceptional child is beyond what we, who have healthy children, can imagine.

And Then We Are Born

On the day of our birth, it has been said that humans have their skulls crushed, limbs dislocated, flesh severed, and eyes assaulted with blinding white light [3]. The physical pain that all humans experience at birth contrasts in unimaginable proportions with the heavenly protective contentment that is experienced in the *forever* of the previous seven months. This ultimate contrast becomes the foundation of the paramount human separation anxiety. We are literally ripped from our God's womb, a Paradise Lost in its truest essence. Torn from the Garden of Eden, we immediately and continually search for ways of re-entering the space from which we were so crudely and completely torn. We instinctively cling to the bosom of our survival. Perhaps, initially, we even fool ourselves into believing that we have re-entered the foundation of our conscious and sub-conscious existence. But soon the bewilderment of returned hunger, renewed fears, and stress take the place of the false sense of permanence, contentment, and safety of our mother's arms. At birth, we become aware, for the first time, of *needs* and *wants*.

Needs and Wants

Although human needs and wants are both physical and psychological, there is, however, a difference between the two. It's not that a need is just a strong want, either. My wife and I would discuss this often in the first years of our marriage, usually in the context of our evolving relationship. My clinical practice helped hone our discussions into a tool that has helped clarify the First Law of Effective Thinking: ***LIFE IS DIFFICULT***.

Wants are only conscious.
Needs are both conscious and unconscious.

If you *want* to eat an ice cream cone and I can get you to think of playing a game of tennis, the *wanted* ice cream cone quietly fades.

But humans, as well as all living things, also have *needs*. We *need* to fulfill Maslow's first two rungs of the hierarchy of needs (food, clothing, warmth, shelter, and safety) or we will become seriously ill and perhaps even die.

We unconsciously pursue these necessary aspects of life, and, if they are not satisfied at the unconscious level, then we seek them consciously. If we do not get food, clothing, warmth, and shelter on the unconscious level, we consciously become obsessed with getting them. Now we are on the survival level and will fulfill our needs or transition from discomfort, perhaps even death.

There are also *psychological* needs and wants, and our emotional survival requires that we obtain them. Being touched and held, recognized first for *who* we are, then for *what* we do, along with being emotionally supported and protected, are *needed* for healthy psychological development and existence on this womb-to-tomb trip that we are all on. The conscious wanting, or not wanting, of these components of social interaction is irrelevant. Humans *need* these for emotional survival, or *The Stir Crazy Sign* will rear its ugly head and make life more miserable than it needs to be.

The total and permanent satiation of needs and wants only occurs in the womb.

Many social and economic systems teach us that if we only provide *this*, or accumulate *that,* we shall overcome the perpetual confusion of what I call our "existence dissonance." The perpetual difference between our in-womb experiences during our Period of Awe and our post-birth search for the tonalities of re-entry into heaven is a lifelong endeavor—a personal crusade that every human attempts to resolve, but inherently is incapable of doing.

Sometimes we temporarily fool ourselves into believing that we have arrived back at that perfect state we so desperately long for: when we're first laid at our mother's breast; when we first slip into a warm, soapy bubble bath or frothing, body-suspending Jacuzzi; or perhaps when we awaken on a cold Saturday morning and realize that we don't have to get up and go to work. We can then curl our legs up into that imprinted fetal position, gather the blankets to our nose, and gently fall back to sleep.

Sooner than we'd ever want, homeostasis or balance is shifted, and our human needs and wants return. We no longer are hungry; we can sleep no longer; we get water-logged.

Unlike our pre-birth experience of perfect and perpetual balance, human attempts for in-life everlasting homeostasis are doomed to failure.

After our birth, and most certainly after language is developed, we can never re-experience what life was like pre-language and pre-logic. This is the major dissonance or communication block among the upper cerebral cortex, the frontal lobe, and the temporal lobe. The temporal lobe (specifically, the hippocampus and the amygdala) experienced *heaven*; neither the frontal lobe nor the cerebral cortex were ever *there*, but perpetually try, on dictates from the amygdala, to translate experiences from language into sensations. Images come forward, but their linguistic descriptions always fall short.

Stained glass windows with beams of Sunday morning light may help; prayer may get us still closer; wishes are begged to come true; but the upper cerebral cortex can't do what the temporal lobe does so exquisitely. The temporal lobe holds on to that perfectionistic memory that had no previous sense of *anything* less than total dependency, vulnerability, and intimacy with the void of all needs and wants.

This quest of obtaining post-womb perfection and satiation of all wants and needs is well described in a paraphrase of the oft-quoted piece written by the Baptist minister, Robert E. Hastings, which he called

The Station - -

Tucked away in our subconscious is an idyllic vision.
We see ourselves on a long trip that spans the continent.

We are traveling by train. Out the windows we drink in the passing
scene of cars on nearby highways, of children waving at a crossing,
of cattle grazing on a distant hillside, of smoke pouring from a
power plant, of row upon row of corn and wheat, of flatlands and
valleys, of mountains and rolling hillsides, of city skylines and
village halls. But uppermost in our minds is the final destination.
On a certain day at a certain hour we will pull into the station.
Bands will be playing and flags waving. Once we get there so many
wonderful dreams will come true and the pieces of our lives will fit
together like a completed jigsaw puzzle.

How restlessly we pace the aisles, cursing the minutes for loitering
waiting, waiting, waiting for the station.

"When we reach the station that will be it we cry."
"When I'm 18!"
"When I buy a new 450SL Mercedes."
"When I put the last kid through college."
"When I pay off the mortgage."
"When I get a promotion."
"When I reach the age of retirement, I shall live happily ever after."

Sooner or later we need to realize there is no Station, no one place
to arrive at once and for all. The true joy of life is the trip. The
station is only a dream. It constantly outdistances us. It isn't the
burdens of today that drive men mad. It is the regrets over yesterday and the fear of tomorrow. Regret and fear are twin thieves who
rob us of today.

Stop pacing the aisles and counting the miles. Instead, climb more
mountains. Eat more ice cream. Go barefoot more often. Swim
more rivers, watch more sunsets. Laugh more. Cry less. Life must
be lived as we go along . . . the STATION will come soon enough.

Re-read Hastings' last line. "The station will come soon enough." The classic interpretation of Robert Hasting's *The Station* is a reference to *death* as the Station for all humans.

However, I propose a different view. What if we came **from** the Station. The irony of *The Station* is that we have already been there.

Few psychologists and psychiatrists ponder this as the most basic source of our strife and struggles. Everyone is a hero in their own life's novel. No two lives are the same, but all normally developed human beings have something in common. Normally developed people experience the perfection to which the temporal lobe, and specifically the amygdala, demands we return. *No one* can *ever* return to where we all came from, that perfect state of being during the last seven months of our gestation called the **Period of Awe**. That place where we were conditioned to experience heaven, when we were with our Maker in paradise; where every inch of our surface was enveloped by the warmth and protection of our Maker; the only time in our human existence when we had no wants or needs; where we were totally dependent, vulnerable, and intimate; the only time in our existence when Life was NOT Difficult.

Hastings is correct when he advises that *"the true joy of life is the trip,"* but even with death being interpreted as the Station, we can never get to *it*. Carl Sagan postulated that "we are matter made conscious" but with death there is the undoing of that matter with the result being the end of consciousness as we know it.

The ventral section of the frontal lobe and the amygdala, or the temporal lobe, may have belief sets about what may or may not occur after we arrive at The Station, but this is barren territory for the upper cerebral cortex. It is painful and difficult for physicians, nurses, hospital workers, and therapists to help people, whom we have grown to know and love, get through *the portal* to Hastings' Station. And, just as no two lives are the same so also, no two periods of dying are the same. In any case, Hastings' Station will come soon enough for us all.

The Trip

Mental health professionals pick up the struggle of *the trip* only after patients are well on their way. We try to figure out how to help people maximize their travels on this womb-to-tomb excursion that we're all on, but few of us consider the essence of the struggle: *How can we re-enter the heaven from where we all came? And what do we do when we realize that we ultimately can't get there?*

A helpful start is to realize that Life is Difficult, **not** because of sins of omission or commission on our part or the part of others, rather Life Is Difficult because it is **supposed** to be.

When everything works right, life will still be **difficult**. How we adapt to this struggle becomes the essence of successful living.

FRIDAY'S LAWS

1. Life Is Difficult.

2. **Perception Is Reality.**

3. Change Is The Toughest Thing A Human Being Can Do.

4. You Can Never Change Another Human Being; You Can Only Change Yourself. When You Change, They Change, But You Can Not Change Them.

5. I Am Responsible For Everything I Do And Say. I Am Not Responsible For Your Response.

6. The Future And The Past Are Seldom As Good Or As Bad As We Anticipate Or Remember.

7. No One Has A Squeaky Clean Psyche.

8. The Only Thing That Lasts Forever Is . . . NOW.

Perception is Reality.

The image will become more important than the object and will, in fact, make the object dispensable.

Oliver Wendell Holmes
commenting on how the world changed with the invention of the photograph

Man is free, but not unless he believes it.

Giacomo Girolamo Casanova DeSeinsalt

Humans function on their perceptions. It doesn't matter if these perceptions are *right* or *wrong*; *good* or *bad*, *intelligent* or *stupid*, *crazy* or *reasonable*. Every human who has ever lived has always functioned on what he or she perceives. Human perceptions are so inherently subjective that each perception is unique to all of human history, and yet we obtain such comfort and solace when we sense *common perceptions* with people we know and trust. Even everyday perceptions like watching sporting events or witnessing an accident are experienced and recalled uniquely. If ten people witness an automobile accident and are interviewed individually, one might think that there were at least five separate mishaps. From the mid-nineteenth century onward, pictures and then film have been able to document what *really* happened. However, instead of clarifying reality, angles, points of view, and even computerized interventions, have cast doubt on our perceptions, which is all that human reality is.

Here are a few examples of *perception* **vs**. *reality*: The first is the classic drawing of two black profiles vs. a white vase.

One may even be able to see both at the same time.

I recall working several years ago with a young man who was diagnosed as having paranoid schizophrenia. We were very early in our working relationship when I mentioned to him the concept that our reality was truly only what our perceptions permitted it to be. The perceptions for someone with paranoid schizophrenia can range from humorous to frightful. Sensing the need for an example, I went over to my bookshelf and pulled down an old psychology text book of mine and opened it to the section on human perception. I showed him a copy of a drawing and asked him what he saw.

He glanced at it, responded quickly, "A young woman looking down to her right," and handed the book back to me.

"Look at it a little longer," I urged.

He took the book back, stared at it awhile, and then exclaimed (with a bit too much excitement),

"Doc, I see it. I see where someone took a knife and slit her throat. Then if you make the slice her very thin lips, the young lady turns into an old witch!"

When our very human perceptions change, our realities change.

Some people, especially harried, fast moving *successful* people, protest that artists' illusions are far from the realities of the real worlds of commerce, homemaking, child rearing, and general lifestyles of the normally non-rich and non-famous. This, I've found, is especially true of people who are locked into the written and spoken language arts, such as lawyers, educators, and writers. Physicians and administrators are notorious for *knowing reality* and often have little patience for anyone who would (might I use the word "dare"?) perhaps perceive something other than their knowledge of *truth* (see the Introduction for the discussion of *truth* as it pertains to *The Stir Crazy Sign*). So, I've been known to offer the following English sentence:

Finished files are the re-
sult of years of scientif-
ic study combined with the
experience of many years.

How many "F's" are there in the sentence above? Please count the total number of "F's" again *slowly*.

When I've proposed this real-life, solid, non-artistic, non-illusional question to both individuals and large groups, I've always received a variety of responses. The answers range from three (most people) to seven. (The answer is at the end of this chapter.) The point is that we as humans **function** on our conscious and unconscious perceptions, and this functioning is displayed in our behaviors throughout our days and lives.

Do you see a dalmatian grazing in a field in the following picture?

Studies of informed consent prior to major surgery have shown a fascinating example of perception being reality. Patients were filmed at bedside being given information about their soon-to-be-performed heart surgery. The patients were all well oriented and appropriately interactive with their medical interviewers. Several days following their surgery, these same patients were asked what they remembered of their pre-surgery conference. Few patients could recall ever being told the pertinent details. When shown the films of their pre-surgery conferences, the patients were, on the whole, incredulous. They certainly were not lying when they said they didn't remember the interviews or the instructions. **Their perceptions were as accurate for them as your perceptions are accurate for you**.

There is a test in Appendix II that you may wish to take at this time. It will give you some insight into how you perceive yourself at this point in Friday's Laws

The psychiatrist R.D. Laing accentuated this principle of perception being reality in his work on schizophrenic thought patterns. In his classic book, *Knots*, Dr. Laing led his readers on a journey into the labyrinth of the torturous, cyclical thinking of paranoid schizophrenics. Dr. Laing gave us a glimpse of what disturbed, abnormal thought patterns are like. As a graduate student in the mid 1970s, I would often marvel at his perceptual insight into the disturbed mind. Later, working with alcoholics, I realized the commonality of all human interactions. Regardless of the number of nurses, psychiatrists, internists, and even dermatologists who would visit a withdrawing alcoholic, all offering their own strong assurances that there were "no ants on your body" the withdrawing alcoholic would often continue with his/her torturous scratching. Where there is conscious and unconscious perception, there is human, mental, and physical reaction. If a medical technologist operating a heart/lung machine during open heart surgery perceives a blood gas reading to be at a particular level, he will alter gauges to regulate it, all according to what he perceives the problem to be. An air traffic controller will change the course of a plane, as would a plumber move a plumbing-snake, on the same principle that . . .

PERCEPTION IS REALITY.

How Perceptions Affect Thinking Effectively

The foundations of Cognitive Behavioral Psychotherapy pro-pose a four-stage flow of human activity:

> **THINKING**
> ⇩
> **EMOTIONS**
> ⇩
> **BEHAVIORS**
> ⇩
> **SYMPTOMS**

How we think leads to how we feel. These feelings, or emo-tions, establish the foundations for our behaviors. It is our human behavior which establishes the symptoms that become the focal point of our social functioning and interactions.

The theory of Cognitive Behavioral Therapy (CBT) postulates that, as we change our thinking, our emotions will change. Change our emotions, and our behaviors will alter. With changed behaviors, the symptoms of our lives will change. (Of course, life is **never** symptom-free.) A great deal of effort is invested in ther-apy to help people change their conscious thinking and recognize destructive thought patterns.

With the current research on the brain's structure and func-tion, the cognitive therapy model of . . .

```
┌─────────────────────────────┐
│                             │
│          THINKING           │
│             ⇩               │
│          EMOTIONS           │
│             ⇩               │
│          BEHAVIORS          │
│             ⇩               │
│          SYMPTOMS           │
│                             │
└─────────────────────────────┘
```

now needs to be modified.

Because of research on the temporal lobe, specifically the components of the amygdala, hippocampus, and hypothalamus (Appendix I), the cognitive therapy model changes to look like this:

```
┌────────────────────────────────────────────┐
│                                            │
│   PRE-COGNITIVE EMOTIONAL REACTIONS        │
│                   ⇩                        │
│                THINKING                    │
│                   ⇩                        │
│                EMOTIONS                    │
│                   ⇩                        │
│                BEHAVIOR                    │
│                   ⇩                        │
│                SYMPTOMS                    │
│                                            │
└────────────────────────────────────────────┘
```

This makes sense. Think of what happens when we hear a sudden loud noise. We jump and then wonder what the noise was. We are beginning to understand how the temporal lobe takes initial survival precedence over the *higher order* of figuring out what the potential life threatening, or ego threatening, sensation was. This is why I metaphorically call the amygdala the "Chicken Little Lobe." These two almond-shaped neuron-packed nuggets are the center of human *fight/flight* responses. Always on sentry duty, these two nodules constantly whisper (or scream) their warnings that "the sky is falling" to heighten the probabilities of survival. The amygdala send out perpetual background static that the frontal lobe and cerebral cortex of patients suffering with anxiety or panic disorders find difficult to turn off.

Those of us blessed with the absence of these anxiety disorders find the occasional flood of the survival fluid of adrenaline a curious life event. With brief self-assurance that we're all right, we get back to the chores of daily life, and later recall to associates and loved ones our *close call* with a perceived threat of a near accident.

The fight/flight reaction **is** initiated with stimuli from all five senses, not just hearing. We automatically react when we touch a hot plate, or taste a strange food. We shut our eyes and turn our heads when we suddenly come upon a gory accident, or wince when we get a whiff of a foul smelling piece of rancid meat. These sensory perceptions are then followed by *Thoughts, Emotions, Behaviors,* and, finally, the *Symptoms* when we screech "ouch!" or when we cough, or when we gag and our stomachs retch.

Neuropsychologists are channeling their efforts toward a better understanding of the amygdala and hippocampus. These two small, but critically important, areas of the brain appear to be a key to our functioning and sense of self. Some researchers are honing their attention on the amygdala as *the soul of the brain*. Spatially, these two, neuronal masses sit just above the upper brain stem. They are just in front of and somewhat below the hippocampus, and on either side of the thalamus (see Appendix I for further description of location and structure).

The five human senses of sight, sound, taste, touch, and smell generate our world and are windows to it. These senses encapsulate all of the external information that is passed into our cerebral cortex. The thalamus is the *modem* or *directory assistance* which transfers the sensory information into our cerebral cortex for *conscious thought*. Sensations, especially the sense of smell, occur preconsciously. The brains of our very early ancestors, compared to our current brain size, were very small. When our brains consisted of not much more than our current brain stem and temporal lobe, we only had what we now call a *smell brain*. Recent research indicates that there still is a direct pathway from the olfactory sense directly into the amygdala. This causes us to have rapid remembering of events and situations long before (in bio-neuro-electrical time) we have higher order cognition as to what those smells and events might be. Harder to retrieve, language-based memories can be rapidly re-lived later after the sense of smell explodes its power directly onto the amygdala. The smell of the extinguished birthday candle can place us at the joyous, or traumatic, events of our fifth birthday party long before we can place the specific descriptions or recollections of the event. The aroma of a grilled hamburger can catapult us to a summer campground of our youth. The scent of a woman on an elevator can place us at our mother's knee. The fragrance of a summer's retreating flower can bring memories of our first day of school. All of these flashbacks occur at an emotional level that precedes our ability to recollect or structure the event in words.

The Rational Human

We humans are not rational, in spite of our egocentric demands to be so. We are *rationalizing*. We obtain conscious and unconscious emotional positions about things, and then give all the reasons why we are right. The great early 20th century American psychologist, William James, said, "A great many people think they are thinking when they are merely rearranging their prejudices." Our prejudices are the deep communications between our temporal lobe and the ventral area of our frontal lobe. When someone agrees with us, we may consider that person to be our friend or compatriot, for he/she is *with us*. Depending on the strength or importance of the issue at hand, or degree of ego or physical threat, there may be a shunning of those who disagree with us. There may even be a fight, a strike, or a multi-generational feud. A crusade or jihad will surely wipe out the *infidels*, those bad, evil, contemptible people, institutions, governments, or nations who dare challenge the *fact* that we are right and they are wrong. A fact that has transitioned from belief through the gray areas of truth and faith into those black and white worlds of fundamentalism, terrorism, and mass suicides (*The Stir Crazy Sign* as described in the Introduction).

We all have conscious perceptions, usually referred to as *thoughts*. More important, though, are pre-conscious perceptions. These pre-conscious thoughts appear to be generated by the temporal lobe and upper brain stem (see Appendix I for location and discussion of brain area functions), the true survival and maintenance areas of the human brain. These two primitive brain areas are the critical cornerstones for the *correct* and *incorrect* thinking patterns that occur *consciously,* i.e., the *higher-order* correct thinking located in the upper cerebral cortex.

Your perceptions are *your* reality. You may cognitively structure a world outside of your perceptions, but your fundamental
interaction with people and things is predicated on the 2nd law of
effective thinking:

PERCEPTION IS REALITY

If you perceive, for example, that climbing a ladder is dangerous, you are going to function as if it is dangerous. If you perceive
that walking an I-beam 2,000 feet above a New York sidewalk is
safe, then you are going to function as if it is safe. If you perceive
that someone is kind and understanding, you will relate to that
person according to your perceptions, even if unbeknown, to you,
that person is a convicted rapist, thief, or mass murderer.

All horror movies and novels are based on the 2nd Law of
Effective Thinking. The reader or viewer perceives the danger of a
devouring monster lurking just around the bend. As you read a
terrorizing passage of a book, or watch an explicitly erotic scene in
a movie, you can notice your heart rate increase. Your temporal
lobe is tricked into believing that you are *actually there* witnessing a
pending horrific experience or a wonderfully sensual vignette.
Through the written word or visual image (a cerebral cortex
stimulus), an expectation of a pending disaster is triggered, and
your temporal lobe responds by telling you to get ready to fight,
flee, faint, or enjoy.

You do not have to be paranoid to perceive the world as being
a dangerous place to live; nor are you *crazy* to perceive it as a safe
place to be. An excellent example of perception vs. reality is
Sandra. Sandra's sense of pain and danger was stored well within
her limbic system, a sense that was reinforced with each of the 37
major facial and cranial operations that she has endured over the
15 years that I have known her.

On a fateful day in the late 1970s, not long after Sandra had left her religious convent, this 20-something-year-old woman was sitting at a table with her friends. She was the right fielder on a women's softball team and, while at a restaurant with her teammates, she took a bite out of an apple and her jaw locked open. Unable to close her mouth, she tried to laugh at the sight of herself with her mouth ajar. It was no laughing matter.

Psycho-dynamic interpretations aside, Sandra began a horrendous journey through the modern medical system. When I first met Sandra,she saw herself as a near-destitute, grotesquely disfigured young woman, who *perceived* herself as almost less than human.

I have had the privilege of knowing Sandra for almost 15 years. I have accompanied her into the operating room for many of her 37 major surgical procedures. These operations have tried to fix her jaw and alleviate the horrific physical pain she endures. What she has learned to do with her perceptions is a marvel of human capabilities. Due to her diminished blood flow (arterial-venous system), she must often undergo *awake intubations*. While she is conscious, a tube is inserted into her lungs by way of her nasal passageway. This is a very painful, and potentially terrifying, experience which she tolerates with amazing calm.

Sandra has learned to use medical hypnosis to augment her anesthetics for all of her surgical procedures. She is able to suspend physically painful assaults on her body. This probably occurs with the combined use of her temporal lobe and upper brain stem. She experiences a *mind-body separation* that is not unrelated to that sensation of excitement you experience when you read an arousing book. It is a fascinating process to witness.

The ability to consciously alter physical and psychological reactions with words is a prodigious acquisition of the well developed human brain. God, grace, or angels may be present, but to watch patients balance *holding on* and *letting go,* in such a way as to let masked people shove plastic tubes down their throats without flinching, is both a marvel and a miracle of the elements of the human brain working together *without The Stir Crazy Sign.*

As humans, our experiences combine with our conscious perceptions to propel us forward in life.

Perceptions are reality.

There are six [6] "F's" in the sentence on page 49.

FRIDAY'S LAWS

1. Life Is Difficult.

2. Perception Is Reality.

3. **Change Is The Toughest Thing A Human   Being Can Do.**

4. You Can Never Change Another Human Being; You Can Only Change Yourself. When You Change, They Change, But You Can Not Change Them.

5. I Am Responsible For Everything I Do And Say. I Am Not Responsible For Your Response.

6. The Future And The Past Are Seldom As Good Or As Bad As We Anticipate Or Remember.

7. No One Has A Squeaky Clean Psyche.

8. The Only Thing That Lasts Forever Is . . . NOW.

3

CHANGE IS THE TOUGHEST THING A HUMAN BEING CAN DO

Human nature will not change. In any future great national trial, compared with the men of this, we shall have as weak and as strong, as silly and as wise, as bad and as good.
Abraham Lincoln

The absurd man is he who never changes.
Marseille Barthelemy

In addition to being human toxic waste dumps, clinical psychologists are *change agents*. For multiple hours of every working day, psychotherapists throughout the industrial world profess to help people accomplish what they are requesting: CHANGE.

After 50,000 hours of professional garbage collecting, I am convinced that, outside of a massive conspiracy, my patients find it excruciatingly difficult to change. Most patients would like to change other people, sometimes MANY other people (see Chapter 4), but self-change is, I am confident, **THE** most difficult thing that humans can do.

When I talk about change I'm not implying hairstyles, occupations, or even mates. The reference is to those innermost, fundamental aspects of **Who** we are. That deep-seated sense of self that swirls around the temporal lobe of the human inner brain where the amygdala (our "Chicken Little Lobe" described in Chapter 2) and the hippocampus reside. When therapeutic change is discussed, we're ultimately *not* thinking of the upper cerebral cortex where *higher order* thought and constructs occur. This may be where the conscious process of psychological change starts, but it is certainly not the end point of therapeutic work. The end point of the work of all therapists is to facilitate changes in the temporal lobe, so there can be balance in brain activity. Consistent domination of one brain section over another causes distress.

Lies, Lies, and More Lies

Eat with the rich, but go to the play with the poor, who are capable of joy.
                 L. Logan Pearsall Smith

Most inhabitants of the industrial world dream of the changes that would take place *if only* their basic economic lives were different. Our internal voices plead for the attainment of the multitude of dreams that would be fulfilled, *if only...*

I hit the lottery;
I meet Mr. or Ms. Right;
If I can get that long-sought-after job or promotion;
If I'm recognized as having produced the perfect child, perfect house, or perfect project;

THEN my life will no longer be difficult.

Many a wealthy Madison Avenue mogul have accumulated the *toys* that represent *winning* in our society by successfully appealing to the temporal lobes of a large group of people. The temporal lobe in every human being *knows* that all eight of *Friday's Laws* are true and correct in the **opposite**.

The *winning* mantra of advertisers throughout the world is: If this product is purchased, that service obtained, or that process experienced, then, AND ONLY THEN, will your life be fulfilled. You will then acquire the biggest and best statements of society's success: the title, the correct path to heaven, the top corner office, the golden parachute; your life will be easy.

Psychology practices throughout the world have had literally hundreds of thousands of patients who have listened to these *lies of materialism*. The proper clinical goal, however, is NOT to extinguish the drive to obtain material things. Rather, it is to help people to *think effectively; to know when they have **crazy** ideas.*

Here is an exercise that you may want to try. Toward the end of our therapeutic relationship, Joann, a former patient of mine, described to me a belief that, at first thought, will certainly seem *crazy* to you, but, as Chapter 6 will illustrate, "Maybe so. Maybe not."

Lotteries and Crazy Ideas

The whole purpose of lotteries and gambling establishments throughout the world is to appeal to the temporal lobe in each of us. We are compelled to believe that there is perpetual happiness (a continual dearth of needs and wants) **if only** the winning ticket were bought; **if only** that magical coin is dropped into that special slot machine; or **if only** that long-lost rich uncle remembers you in his last will and testament.

Joann lived in Pennsylvania where there is a state lottery. Only when there is more than $25 million in the Lottery Jackpot did Joan *lease* her very own fantasy (versus just buying a ticket). She always purchased four tickets, one each for both of her children, one for her husband, and one for herself. She would buy the four tickets as early as she could and place them under a magnet on the side of the refrigerator. She then began to fantasize. Joann described to me in detail all of the things that she would do with her new wealth.

Oh, the showering of (unearned) respect that she'd get! A life filled with such wonderful changes would befall her.

Joann then related how, within a couple of days, a growing sense of melancholy would begin to descend upon her. Although she certainly was not wealthy (always aware of the 2nd Law that Perception is Reality), Joann and her husband were comfortable. They had a comfortable home, healthy children, and a lifestyle that permitted them to give to others.

However, Joann believed that her lifestyle would dramatically change with the sudden winning of the state lottery. I would remind her that *change,* regardless of whether it is a positive or negative change, *is the most difficult thing a human being can do.* This is especially true if the change is directed or controlled by outside forces, as would happen with *unlimited* wealth.

How would Joann's colleagues relate to her if they knew that she, unlike most of them, didn't have to work? Harry, Joann's husband, certainly couldn't function the way he did as a high school teacher in a local public school district. Most school boards and employers would find it difficult having an employee that could buy and sell them several times over if that employee didn't function or behave in the way they wanted them to. And yet Harry loved to teach children.

Joann's best friend, Sally, was an unemployed secretary. Would she remain her best friend? Would Joann wonder how many new *friends* and relatives she would suddenly acquire with her nouveau riche status?

My patient was a member of a prestigious golf club located south of Pittsburgh in the small town in which her family lives. She had often described the other members' intense superficiality and pomposity, much of which was due to their perception of having wealth. Joann related how many people who belonged to her Club believed that their *crazy ideas weren't crazy,* with the concomitant behaviors that were often embarrassing to everyone involved. Joann began to observe that wealth not only severely complicated life, but also, fundamentally, did not do a thing to change the 1st Law (Life is Difficult.). The lives of wealthy people were still difficult, even though people without wealth always seem to find this concept enigmatic.

As the days marched on, and the Saturday night drawing of Joann's winning lottery number got closer and closer, her cerebral cortex **let** her temporal lobe continue with the fantasy that she had bought the winning ticket of her pending unlimited wealth. Her upper cerebral cortex went so far as to let Joann's temporal lobe *know* that she had WON the lottery. No, she didn't go out and buy a new Mercedes or make an appointment with a real estate agent to buy a new house. She did, however, allow (force) her fantasy to proceed.

I mentioned earlier that she *leased* the fantasy. While Joann *bought* the four lottery tickets, she only *leased* the fantasy of winning. Joann would keep her fantasy going by not watching the actual lottery drawing on Saturday night. She therefore could have additional dreams without any additional cost.

Joann didn't check the number on Sunday; she didn't check it on Monday; not even on the Tuesday after the lottery drawing. Why should she, when her temporal lobe *knew* that she had already won the big prize?

Now comes the behavior that many will consider *crazy*. Joann took the four tickets and threw them in the kitchen garbage can. She threw them away without ever checking whether she had won anything or not.

For Joann, *winning* wasn't the purpose of *leasing* the fantasy in the first place. The purpose of spending her $4 was to have her upper cerebral cortex monitor her temporal lobe. Joann used this exercise (and I assume that she continues to do this today) to observe the level of control and influence her temporal lobe has over effective living. Joann's upper cerebral cortex also calculated the mathematical odds of winning a $25 million state lottery. With the chances at one in many, many million, Joann knew that she was more likely to be struck by lightning several times on the same day than to win the lottery. Joann's temporal lobe was the brain section that *knew* she was an instant multi-millionaire.

Joann and I often discussed that it would take a lot more than reading Hastings' *The Station,* and memorizing the "Laws of Effective Thinking" to change the embedded delusion that wealth provides the means for making life easy. Swirling deep inside the **temporal lobe** is a critically important concept: the 1st Law, as well as the remaining seven Laws, are without question or exception *true and correct **in the opposite***. The goal of Thinking Effectively is **NOT** to change the temporal lobe into something that it isn't, namely a logical, reasonable entity that thinks and resolves life's cursory problems. Effective thinking understands that the driving energy of life itself is the brain stem and the temporal lobe.

The goal of effective thinking is to have the upper cerebral cortex (where the areas of logic and reason are located) maintain a smidgen more energy or power than the temporal lobe, where deep, fight/flight emotions reside, or the ventral area of the frontal lobe (where our learned values are stored). The rationale behind this aspiration is to allow major life decisions to be administered by the upper cerebral cortex, and **not** by these other two brain sections.

Changing your view of money, and its role in your life, may be one of the more difficult things that you ever do; *and* one of the most important.

The Struggle of Adaptation

Life can be described as the *struggle of adaptation*. People who do not adapt have lives that are more difficult than they need to be. To consciously change the way we think though, to alter our beliefs, to modify over time our attitudes and behaviors, can be a very painful process. And psychotherapy certainly is no *quick fix*. That is why this book, as stated in the Introduction, is **not** meant to be a quick fix *self- help* cookbook.

This book will make your life easier, but it will not fix a deep-seated emotional problem. *This book describes the human condition when it works right.* If change were easy, doctors, therapists, and preachers would simply stand on street corners and distribute cards with the *Eight Laws of Effective Thinking*. These cards would be given to anyone and everyone who would take one. And if change were easy, it would be done by simply reading the back cover of this book.

Even when it seems the *right* or sensible thing to do, changing **who** we are, which gets displayed in **what** we do, is the most difficult thing we humans do. Change runs counter to the temporal lobe directives for survival. After all, if we have survived this long doing whatever we do, to alter ourselves could lead to our death. The prime directive of the temporal lobe that is functioning correctly is to survive at all costs. And survival, as dictated by the temporal lobe, won't be permanently secured until we get back to that pre-birth perfection that we all experienced in the Period of Awe (see Chapter 1).

For their long-term good, thieves know they shouldn't steal; addicts know they shouldn't inject drugs; alcoholics know they shouldn't drink; parents know they shouldn't harm their children; and seasoned therapists know they shouldn't **should** on their patients. Then why do human beings continue to do things that others can so clearly see are self-destructive, or non-helpful, and **why** is fundamental change the toughest thing a human being can do?

As I mentioned above, the altering of the temporal lobe is a form of personality suicide. To become someone whom we currently are not is anathema to our existence. There is an internal, unconscious psychological directive to stay as we are. For normally developed humans, the temporal lobe is imprinted with the indelible, non-language memory of how perfect existence was during the last seven months of our gestation; how perfect the Period of Awe was when we were in heaven; when there were no wants or needs that needed instantaneous satisfaction; when we had total dependency, total vulnerability, and total intimacy. Were we to change, we may never get ourselves back to the nirvana from whence we come.

There are also external forces that try to keep us from changing. Mothers want their children to stay with them; people don't want their life-long neighbors to move; desperate children beg their physicians to give their dying parent back to them.

One reason change is so difficult to accomplish is that people who know others, and even profess to love these people, don't want their loved ones to change. Even if behaviors are harmful to themselves and to others, *changing is the toughest thing a human being can do.*

Constellations

Imagine how, for millennium after millennium, people have gazed up into the heavens. For thousands of years, humans have mapped the constellations. Groups and clusters of stars have been woven into shepherd stories and songs; star positions have foretold the changing seasons; stars and constellations have guided travelers on their journeys for eons.

Metaphorically, we humans are all stars in the psychic maps of all the people we know and have ever encountered. For most people with whom we come in contact, we are but faint puffs of unknown, gaseous matter. But, for others, for those who know us well, we are guiding stars aiding in our loved ones' emotional security and journeys. They depend on things (and us) staying as they are for their own emotional stability.

How would a shepherd feel if he went outside one starry night, gazed up to the heavens, and found that the North Star had shifted due west? To say that he would be disoriented would be an understatement. And he would, if he could, do everything in his power to get things back to how they were so that his life would not be disrupted. Forget the needs—let alone wants—of other human beings. Keeping our lives as normal and regulated as possible is a directive of the temporal lobe.

Research has shown that humans have emotional recognitions that are lodged in and retrieved from deep within the temporal lobe. These memories are most strongly triggered by the olfactory sense. Our sense of smell registers and creates emotional retrievals and reactions long before our upper cerebral cortex can assign words to these recollections. The whiff of cookies from a bakery fan can place us back in our grandmother's kitchen *before* we can conjure up the words to describe the memories. But the remaining four senses also help solidify memories that keep us on our life path with resistance to change.

Brad, another patient with whom I had the pleasure of working several years ago, related memories of summers that he spent at the Lake Erie shore.

As a nine-year-old boy, the ringing of a telephone only meant disaster for him. When his Aunt Kay would hear the phone ring, she would immediately make a series of rapid signs-of-the-cross. An accident must have occurred or someone surely must have died if the phone rang. Brad's description of his Aunt Kay made me think of Pavlov's dog long before I ever heard of the 1904 Nobel prize winning physiologist.

Brad not only hated phones, but was increasingly agoraphobic (fear of being away from home). He desperately wanted to change. He *knew*, at least intellectually, that the sound of a phone ringing did not necessarily mean disaster, and that Lake Erie was no scarier or less safe than was Pittsburgh, one hundred twenty miles to the south of Erie. But just because his upper cerebral cortex *knew* something, didn't necessarily mean that the concept was translated down into his temporal lobe.

Phobias and Anxieties

The deep-seated insecurities of agoraphobics are excellent examples of sensory stimulation causing physical and psychological responses of major life-disrupting proportions. People suffering from phobias live with a terrible human affliction. They become prisoners of their own brains, immobilized from the daily functioning that you and I take for granted. The process of changing the temporal lobe, where all fears wallow, through the efforts of the logical and reasonable section of the cerebral cortex is the toughest thing a human can do, and is the stuff of cognitive psychotherapy.

As any phobic can tell you, admonitions, directives, and cajoling are useless exercises in the removal of deep seated fears. It is another example of *The Stir Crazy Sign* (see the Introduction), where the ventral section of the frontal and the temporal lobes are going around and around while excluding the logical, problem-solving section of the upper cerebral cortex.

Some time ago I was consulted to work with a woman whom we will call Kathryn. She had been admitted to our hospital for a hysterectomy, and post-operatively, while still in a semi-conscious state, was placed on the fifth floor of our hospital, where our post-surgical patients are routinely cared for.

Unfortunately, Kathryn was a severe claustrophobic, and, when the time came to leave the hospital, she was virtually paralyzed with fright at the thought of getting into an elevator. A true dilemma was evolving.

She began to cry hysterically and shout that she was having a heart attack. It had been over 20 years since she had been on an elevator. She also understood that her post-operative condition made her incapable of taking the steps down to her waiting car.

Our solution was to help her change her perceptions (2nd Law) so that her world would change (3rd Law). She had agreed to use hypnosis to alter her sensation of claustrophobia.

Within 10 minutes of being induced into a hypnotic trance, Kathryn sat in her car ready to be taken home to recover from her surgery. Although medical hypnosis was **not** Kathryn's solution for her claustrophobia, it had helped with her immediate symptom.

About six weeks after her operation, Kathryn and I met in the lobby of my office building. In a quiet corner of the first floor, Kathryn described how she, as a nine-year-old girl, saw the lid of her father's casket being closed. That was the last time she had ridden on an elevator. After 15 minutes of doing what the Epilogue describes as *the therapeutic process*, Kathryn took her second ride on an elevator in 30 years. We got on the elevator, her mind's moving casket, and she squeezed me so hard that the air was forced out of my lungs. When the doors opened on the fifth floor, she walked out and I had her repeat, "That is an elevator; it is neither my father's nor my own casket."

Kathryn was beginning to understand that a *crazy idea of hers was crazy*. She was realizing that normal people have crazy ideas throughout the day. After all, the creation of crazy ideas is the primary task of the temporal lobe. However, normal people know a little quicker when their crazy ideas are crazy.

Successful Living Is NOT to *NOT* Have Crazy Ideas.

For the next 45 minutes, Kathryn and I rode every elevator in the building, all 18 of them—small ones, large ones, empty and crowded ones. Freight elevators and even the elevator that goes to the helicopter pad on the roof were fair game for Kathryn. She even called her daughter and sister from the nurse's station on the seventh floor, the top of the hospital. This was the highest she had been in a building in over 30 years, and although she thanked me, we'll see in Chapter 5 that I certainly was not responsible for her change in behavior.

The Neurotic Delusion of Control (NDC)

Our upper cerebral cortex knows that death is the price we pay for living. There are no values in this concept. It is not a question of right or wrong, good or bad, appropriate or inappropriate, rather a fact of life.

Seventy-six *billion* humans have lived on this earth since man stood erect. Almost six billion people are alive as this book is being written. More people are alive today than have ever been alive at any one time, but, in all probability (see Chapter 6), more people will be alive in the future than are alive today.

Our upper cerebral cortex tells us that all future people, as well as ourselves, will be dead. However, our temporal lobe, that deep-seated part of our pre-conscious existence that was formed between the eighth and ninth week of gestation, KNOWS that we will **never** die.

There are no agonizing emotions in the section of the upper cerebral cortex that houses logic and reason. Death is the price that all living things pay for living. The upper cerebral cortex is not confused by the values of the ventral section of the frontal lobe nor the fight/flight directives of the temporal lobe. It is in the upper cerebral cortex that the Eight Laws of Effective Thinking reside. As far as the concept of death, the upper cerebral cortex knows that it doesn't matter if we're discussing sequoias or sala-manders, grass or grasshoppers, mosquitoes or humans. If it is alive, it WILL die; if it is dead, it WAS alive. This section of the upper cerebral cortex knows that humans ultimately do not control things. The very important things in life are beyond human control. Heart attacks, cerebral hemorrhages, drunks crossing the middle of the road, scud missiles coming through windows, floors collapsing and the millions of other things that humans ponder and fret over are all basically beyond us. These life issues are continually fought over by the upper cerebral cortex (just what *is* going on, and what is the best way of either fixing it or enduring it?), the frontal lobe (what should, has to, better, got to happen if we are to endure, survive, or fix this?), and the temporal lobe (the sky is falling, we're going to die, what will it take to win and live forever in the bliss of the Period of Awe and get away from this difficult life?).

The upper cerebral cortex knows that living reasonable lives will minimize disasters and will raise the probability of forestalling our demise. But, ultimately, this section of the human brain knows that we are not in charge.

The Neurotic Delusion of Control (NDC), however, is not bound by the logic and reason of the northernmost section of the cranium. As long as the NDC is intact, we can swing our feet out of bed and not check to see if the floor is there. When we begin to lose the NDC, or if it gets a little frayed around the edges, anxiety and depressive symptoms begin to raise their proverbial ugly heads. Pain, chronic illness, or sudden losses can all contribute to a reduction of the NDC.

A function of the cerebral cortex is NOT to get the temporal lobe to recognize the *fact* that death is inevitable; that we will never again live in the total safety of our mothers' wombs; that life **IS** difficult. Rather, the prime directive of the logical and reasonable part of our being is to protect and nurture the temporal lobe so as to keep the NDC intact. The *balance* among these three sections of the brain—the upper cerebral cortex, the frontal lobe, and the temporal lobe—is an ideal goal of effective living.

It is deep within the temporal lobe, specifically in the amygdala, that this fundamental structure of everlasting self resides. This deep-seated brain section is the physical location where the **Neurotic Delusion of Control** is also located.

The Delusion of Control is called *Neurotic* because the temporal lobe is the seat and source of our illogical or crazy ideas. That is the job or function of the temporal lobe; to create, as long as we are alive, crazy ideas. Emotions were never meant to be sane nor reasonable. When everything is functioning as it should, we will have ideas about our sense of self, safety, sex and sanity that are *crazy*. The Neurotic Delusion of Control is a critical and necessary part of our daily functioning. But it is up to the upper cerebral cortex, with logic and reason as its boundaries, to sort issues and events into degrees of probabilities and possibilities. The temporal lobe, residence of the NDC, need not concern itself with limitations.

Successful living is not the absence of crazy ideas. Successful living is defined as knowing a little quicker when our crazy ideas are crazy.

Recognizing and changing these crazy ideas into something more viable and rewarding is one of the noble efforts of life.

Change Is The Toughest Thing A Human Being Can Do.

FRIDAY'S LAWS

1. Life Is Difficult.

2. Perception Is Reality.

3. Change Is The Toughest Thing A Human Being Can Do.

4. **You Can Never Change Another Human Being; You Can Only Change Yourself. When You Change, They Change, But You Can Not Change Them.**

5. I Am Responsible For Everything I Do And Say. I Am Not Responsible For Your Response.

6. The Future And The Past Are Seldom As Good Or As Bad As We Anticipate Or Remember.

7. No One Has A Squeaky Clean Psyche.

8. The Only Thing That Lasts Forever Is . . . NOW.

YOU CAN NEVER CHANGE ANOTHER HUMAN BEING.
YOU CAN ONLY CHANGE YOURSELF.
ONCE YOU CHANGE, THEY CHANGE,
BUT YOU CAN NOT CHANGE THEM.

Fortunately, psychoanalysis is not the only way to resolve our inner conflicts. Life itself remains a very effective therapist.
Karen Horney

God, give us grace to accept with serenity the things that cannot be changed, the courage to change the things which should be changed, and the wisdom to distinguish the one from the other.

Reinhold Niebhur

There is a common misconception that good therapists, efficient teachers, competent prisons, and diligent, caring parents can *change* other people. Real change (see Chapter 3) is an intensely internal process that may be influenced by others but is never caused by someone else. True change occurs inside, at the level of the temporal lobe, and can only be guided by the influences of the upper cerebral cortex and the frontal lobe. External forces contribute to change, but far less than what we often believe.

Here is an illustrative story about the effort to change others and the basic futility of that task. In the early 1970s, I was a full-time graduate student at the University of Pittsburgh. During the day, I worked as a school counselor in three small parochial grade schools in the city of Pittsburgh through what was called the Allegheny County Intermediate Unit.

One of the schools to which I was assigned, St. Regis, was certainly a favorite of mine. St. Regis epitomized the dreams of parents for their children. The students from St. Regis parish came from hard working, ethnic families who took great pride in their children's welfare and education. The principal, Sister Michele O'Leary, an inspiring nun from the Mercy Order, approached me soon after I began working at the school.

"Paul, there's lots to do, but you have a special project," she said with more than a hint of a well-maintained Irish brogue. She placed a firm, loving hand (I did catch the paradox) around the shoulder of a handsome 12-year-old boy and drew him next to her.

"Take this boy and get his mind off football and onto books. Motivate him. Get him onto the road that will make him a successful scholar, and get him away from sports. Academic success leads to possibilities. A football goes a hundred yards and stops."

So I met with the boy weekly for the next two years. We'd throw the football around a little, then do some math and reading. I'd always interject Sister Michele's directive. My job was to change this young man.

"You have to pick the right road. The odds and percentages of you going anywhere with football are not good. The chances of you succeeding with hard work and study are much better."

Many well-intentioned parents, teachers, and counselors have been mouthing these same words for decades. As a grade school counselor in my middle twenties, my charge was to facilitate a healthy change in this boy. How else to tell him the correct thoughts than with a loving and guiding hand?

Fortunately, Danny Marino[5] never listened to me. And I learned a great lesson about trying to change people.

Winning

But Danny Marino wins **not** because of his football-playing abilities or financial earning power; Danny Marino wins when he *perspectivizes* his life. When he realizes that his family is what is truly important to him, he is most content. In short, Danny Marino is no different than you are. The best periods for both of you occur when you are able to keep your perspective on the difference between **who you are** and **what you do**. That is what Danny Marino didn't know as a child growing up in Pittsburgh's tough South Oakland, but understands as a man in Miami.

*That is precisely what winning people do well. Winners understand intrinsically that **who** they are is far more important than **what** they do . . .*

Saving People

Mental health professionals are supposed to be change agents. Too often, they are sought out as *rescuers*. Yet when it gets down to the nitty-gritty of changing other people, I reflect on a concept that I learned early on in graduate school. It has been of immense help with both my clinical practice and my life in general. It is called "The Karpman Triangle" and involves the concepts of victims, persecutors and rescuers.

Imagine you are sitting at home one evening and you hear the man next door physically assaulting his wife. She begins to scream for help. What would you do?

Most people would call the authorities, though there certainly are a modicum of people who follow the social policy of "don't get involved." But let's say that you, in fact, do get involved, and you call the police before anything happens:

Who is the Victim? (wife)
Who is the Persecutor? (husband)

Stage I of the Karpman Triangle

RESCUER

Police Officer/You

VICTIM   **PERSECUTOR**

Wife   Husband

The policeman enters the room and grabs the husband.
Now—who becomes the victim? (the husband)

(Who is the persecutor? The police officer [or you])

Stage II of The Karpman Triangle

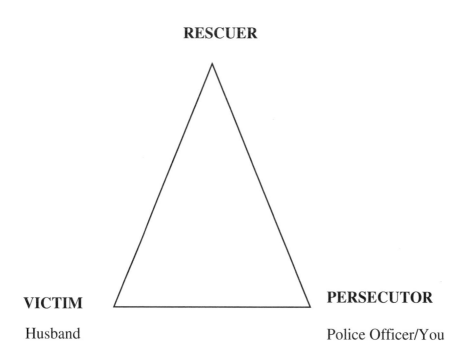

RESCUER

VICTIM

Husband

PERSECUTOR

Police Officer/You

A great irony of human social interactions now ensues. The wife, often with great indignation, begins to scream at the police officer [and you]. "Mind your own business. Get your hands off my husband!"

The wife now becomes the Rescuer!

It is about now that the husband grabs the police officer's gun and shoots him. As he lies bleeding on the kitchen floor,

Who is the Victim? (the police officer [or you])
Who is the Persecutor? (the husband)
Who is the Rescuer? (the medics, minister, and/or under-taker)

Stage III of The Karpman Triangle
Rescuers are viewed as persecutors and end up victims.

RESCUER

Medics/Minister/Undertaker

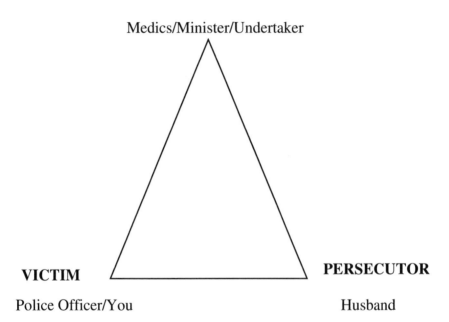

VICTIM   **PERSECUTOR**

Police Officer/You   Husband

Even in situations less drastic or dangerous as the above illustration, be very careful about *rescuing* people. More often than not, your efforts at trying to change someone else will not only fail, but the effort could leave **you** feeling like the victim.

The Karpman Triangle is **not** an endorsement for non-involvement in others' struggles and situations. Rather, it is a caution that if you try to rescue people from their problems, more often than not you will be seen as either an intruder or as a manipulator. People with good intentions can end up being victims.

Interacting Laws of Correct Thinking

As will be revealed, the Laws of Effective Thinking are inter-twined, and reflect back on one another. As an example, this 4th Law—you can only change yourself and once you change, others change, but you cannot change them—reflects back to the 2nd Law (perception *is* reality). As we grow and collect life experiences, we constantly evolve into ever-changing modifications of our *original* self. As we change our perceptions of ourselves and our worlds, we change the three cornerstones of conscious life: cognition, values, and emotions (located in the upper cerebral cortex, frontal lobe, and temporal lobe, respectively).

An example of this evolution and interaction of several of the Laws is the account of Amy and David. Amy was a middle-aged, attractive woman who had accompanied her husband David to my office early one winter morning. Amy and David were the parents of four healthy children. They had no more than the usual financial difficulties for a couple in their position. They both professed love for each other. Physically, David had been examined by a urologist whose judgement I trusted. There was nothing physically wrong that could account for his problem.

The couple had traveled some distance from Ohio in search of a resolution to David's sexual problems. David had lost almost all interest in sexual activity and had great difficulty becoming sexually aroused. (I had already seen David alone several times prior to this meeting, and he appeared to be comfortable in searching for a solution to his problem.) However, there was something uneasy about the way Amy interacted with me. Her answers to questions were curt. Her mood projected anger. She rarely looked me in the eyes. David appeared to have an honest, vested interest in recovering his libido and sexual functioning. I was not sure about Amy.

Amy had been trying to *fix* David. She was increasingly frustrated and angry at her inability to make his problem go away. I was becoming convinced that his passive and decreasing interest in her physically was a statement of him and not her. Her perception of their problem was what she had been focusing on (2nd Law), and she had been trying to change him (4th Law). She was becoming exasperated at her inability to do so. After all, she was office manager of a large computer firm, took care of their four children, and even managed to organize several church-related events with a minimum of help from anybody else. She saw herself as a fixer. She saw him as the one thing that stood in her way of completing her mosaic of being a complete and successful American woman.

As the life story of Amy and David evolved in front of me, I was again reminded of a quote from H.L. Mencken: "For every human problem, there is a solution that is simple, neat, and ... *wrong*." To treat the human condition and the very complex life problems that spin out of intimate relationships simplistically is to ask for trouble. The point here is to show how complex problems intertwine throughout life. Each solution inevitably leads to another set of problems. These newly evolved problems require a different set of adaptations. By utilizing cognition vs. dominating values and emotions, this couple was able to begin thinking about themselves and their problems with a different perspective. They began to know quicker when their crazy ideas were crazy.

Within a few weeks, Amy and David began implementing some of the following *Rules For Fighting* which I developed. These rules are intended for couples where there is an absence of abuse and a strong desire to stay together.

RULES FOR FIGHTING

1. Stick to the point or issue.
2. Don't bring up the past.
3. Feel what the other person is feeling (empathy).
4. Develop a code word, so that when it is employed you immediately back off, and give the other person distance. Use it sparingly; don't violate it.
5. Don't collect Brown Stamps (remember the Gold stamps).
6. When enough distance has been achieved (24 hours?), discuss the issue or problem. This is not to be confused with restarting the argument.
7. If you feel the other person has given in, or has listened to your side of the issue, thank that person. (In relationships, like in business partnerships, both individuals often feel that they give, or work, 75% of the time, with the other giving or working 25% of the time. If everyone *gives in* 55% of the time, there will be fewer battles lost.)
8. Occasionally, switch positions in the middle of the argument.
9. Remember, it is better to have someone to fight with than not to have anyone at all.

What evolved was not a simplistic view of a domineering wife and a passive-aggressive husband, but a complex picture of a couple who had never learned some simple guidelines for fighting. When these guidelines were combined with the framework of what we've covered so far in this work, (namely, that life is supposed to be difficult even *when everything is working right*; that different perceptions do not inherently connote that one person is *right* and the other person is *wrong*; that changing is not impossible but is very difficult for *all* normal human beings and that people can not change other people, but only when they change themselves, so do others change) some very interesting things began to happen in their lives.

Not only did David and Amy's sexual relationship improve greatly, they found themselves wanting to spend more time with each other. They began to balance their business and extracurricular activities in a much healthier way. Their lives continued to be difficult, for the goal of our work together was not to create symptom-free living; only people in morgues and cemeteries are symptom-free. However, their Delusion of Control was back where it should be, and they were no longer seeking to change each other. . .

You Can Never Change Another Human Being, You Can Only Change Yourself; Once You Change, They Change, But You Cannot Change Them.

FRIDAY'S LAWS

1. Life Is Difficult.

2. Perception Is Reality.

3. Change Is The Toughest Thing A Human Being Can Do.

4. You Can Never Change Another Human Being; You Can Only Change Yourself. When You Change, They Change, But You Can Not Change Them.

5. **I Am Responsible For Everything I Do And Say. I Am Not Responsible For Your Response.**

6. The Future And The Past Are Seldom As Good Or As Bad As We Anticipate Or Remember.

7. No One Has A Squeaky Clean Psyche.

8. The Only Thing That Lasts Forever Is . . . NOW.

5

I Am Responsible for Everything I *DO* and *SAY.* I Am *NOT* Responsible for Your Response.

We make a living from what we get. We make a life from what we give. What we have done for ourselves dies with us. What we have done for others and the world is immortal.
George Eliot

O f all of the concepts that delineate Effective Thinking this is, by far, the most difficult to grasp and internalize.

Our Judeo-Christian ethic abhors the thought that we are NOT our brother's keeper; that we are NOT responsible for our children, co-workers, subordinates, church, etc., etc. More therapy time is spent with patients trying to wrestle with this point than with all other issues combined. I am convinced that there are more non-organic psychological and sociological pathologies grounded in the *opposite* of this Law than in all the other Laws of Effective Thinking. People often think, incorrectly, that they are responsible for other people's responses to them, and that other people are responsible for their responses. The realization that people are responsible for their own responses to situations and events is a very difficult concept for many people to comprehend.

Several years ago, a patient offered the following phrase that may help clarify the dilemma of the Fifth Law:

Someone else may be 100% to blame for the conditions under which you struggle, but YOU are 100 % responsible for how you react to them.

Here is an example to illustrate the concept of the 5th Law:

Imagine you are in a room with three other people whom you know rather well. You are not necessarily the best of friends, but you certainly are not strangers to one another.

You say something like: "The mayor of our town is a crook and a thief."

Imagine the responses to this single statement if one of the three people in the room is the mayor's devoted younger brother, one is the mayor's recently defeated opponent in a close, nasty election, and the third person is the town's district attorney.

Responses to this one sentence, that the mayor is considered to be a tainted person, could have a variety of responses:

Perhaps rage.
Perhaps agreement.
Perhaps curious interest.

Three entirely different responses to one statement. Additionally, especially to the stronger reactions, the reactive statements may even be:
"You really make me angry."
"I'm delighted you feel that way also!"
"I'm curious. Can you prove this?"

Those are three very different reactions and responses to one statement.

No human being makes another human being feel anything.
Our feelings are our own.

We have to "own" our feelings if we are ever going to be able to do anything about them. (See Chapter 3 to see why this is so inherently difficult to do.) As long as you think that someone else is responsible for what you think, feel, and/or do, then that person or those people have more influence on you and your life than he or she deserve(s). **You are responsible not only for your responses but also, more importantly, for your life.**

Initially, you may feel better blaming someone else for what you have done, what you have said, or the situation that you are in. But the abdication of responsibility for both who we are and what we do with our lives, ultimately, is the source and foundation of a great deal of human anxiety and depression.

Our reactions to things are statements of us, not of the people or things with which we're dealing.

You Make Me Feel . . .

Several years ago, a patient of mine reflected on a TV commercial he had seen the night before one of our sessions. There had been an attorney of some local repute who had arranged for a series of self-promoting advertisements on several local TV stations. At the end of each commercial, the attorney would look directly into the camera, point his finger at the unseen audience, and say, "We'll get money for **you!**"

Ralph, my patient, offered the insight that there were more fingers on the attorney's hand pointing at himself than there were pointing at the camera. "Perhaps that is why the lawyer was smiling so much," he said.

Ralph's projected insight into this lawyer's possible motives can be placed into the context of this 5th Law of Effective Thinking. When we strongly feel that someone else is responsible for what we feel, in reality we are pointing three times as many fingers at ourselves than we are at them. Reflect on the number of fingers that are pointing at ourselves when we point at others and say, "You make me so happy (angry, sad, etc.)!" This realization gives us the chance to *own* our responses to others. Only when we recognize that our responses to someone or something are statements of ourselves, and not the responses of others or the world we live in, can we do something about it. The upper cerebral cortex knows that other people don't make us feel *anything*. Of course, we all have feelings, but these feelings, like the behaviors that display these feelings, are statements of *ourselves*, *NOT* the person who we initially want to blame or thank.

Art Appreciation

Here is another example of the 5th Law. Let's place you in front of a famous work of art. You remark about what a beautiful painting it is. You are *not* making a statement about the painting. You are making a statement about yourself. Your tastes, values, artistic sense of proportion, color, and shape, and degree of enjoyment, pleasure, or disgust are on display. You may or may not be seeking approval of others with your remarks, but one thing is certain: Your statements and reactions to the painting are not remarks about the painting, nor the world around you. Your statement about the work of art is a statement about you. This is why many people are reluctant to express their views or to take a stand on an issue. Many people do not want to be judged for fear of either making a mistake or being rejected. (A fact that may be reminiscent of our *ejection/rejection* at our birth which is discussed in Chapter 1).

Abulia

Taken to an extreme, people who constantly fear, and then abdicate responsibility for their responses, can contract and display a serious psychiatric disorder called *abulia*. People suffering from abulia live tormented lives. People living with people who have abulia may apply for, and may even be granted, the "Saint of the Year" award. Sufferers of abulia can not make decisions. The selection of clothes to wear, food to eat, places to visit, or things to do create paralyzing and agonizing situations for these people. They abhor taking responsibility for even the most innocuous choices that you and I take for granted throughout the day. Their mantra becomes, "whatever."

Several years ago, I worked with a patient who would agonize for a good 10 minutes at the end of each session about whether to take the 2:00 or the 3:00 appointment the next week. Alice would stammer and stutter. She would fall silent and stare out the window. She would do anything and everything that she could to have me make the decision for her. One can only imagine what her family went through on a daily basis, living with the effects of her malady.

Thankfully, Alice eventually solved her disorder and was able to go about living a relatively normal life. She was able to take responsibility for her life without fixating on other people's responses to her decisions. In the end, her family was as relieved as she was to have her bout with abulia behind her.

The primary goal of the 5th Law is to help gain insight as to where responsibility for our responses truly lies. This upper cerebral cortex concept, which is bound in language and logic, understands the power of owning our responses to stimuli. The temporal lobe, where the deep emotions of fight/flight are lodged, **KNOWS** that other people not only make us feel things, but they are responsible for these emotions.

Before the 5th Law is explained further, a serious caveat to this Law needs to be discussed. *We are always responsible for what we do and say (and what we don't do and don't say)*. If we are aware that someone is going to have a particular reaction to something we are about to do or say, we can *not* nonchalantly say something without owning the potential consequences. Our obligation, if we are asked, is to explain and clarify why we do what we do, or say what we say— always being cognizant that we, as a species, tend to rationalize, not to be rational. We all adopt emotional positions about things and then give the reasons why we are *right* or *correct*.

The 5th Law does not, by any stretch of the imagination, deny emotional reactions. The essence of the temporal lobe has been with us much longer than reason has. Anthropologically speaking, the temporal lobe has been with Homo sapiens for almost 120 million years. The upper cerebral cortex, the crucible of language and logic, has only been a recent addition. With just 30 to 40 million years of development, the upper cerebral cortex is still in its relative infancy. The frontal lobe, a section of which Phineas Gage had blown away 150 years ago, where our values are stored, is even younger than that. Frontal lobe development began to excel about 50,000 years ago. Soon after the Neanderthal became extinct, man's frontal skull began to bulge forward to house this front part of our brains.

In spite of what we would like to believe and have happen, we react emotionally before we think logically. However, if we *own* our emotional reactions as statements of ourselves—and not just statements of our observations of the world we live in—if we take responsibility for our emotional reactions—we will ultimately live more effective lives.

All normal people have crazy ideas every day, all day long.

The 5th Law simply points out that our responses are statements of us and our perceptions (see Chapter 2), and these responses say little or nothing of the world we live in. Our temporal lobe will NEVER accept, nor comprehend this, for the developmental Period of Awe—the last seven months of normal gestation (see the Introduction)—had NO sense of responsibility for responses. Everything was *caused* by our mother, and our mother WAS responsible for everything we sensed. All of our proverbial plates were empty. There were no regrets or fears. It was heaven with no needs or wants, and no responsibility for or from anyone.

The goal of Effective Living is not to deny emotional responses, nor is it to transform the temporal lobe into some form of the higher cerebral cortex functioning. The goal of Effective Living is to understand the directives of the temporal lobe with the upper cerebral cortex *thinking effectively—knowing when we have crazy ideas.*

After all, *normal people as well as crazy people have crazy ideas.* The only difference between the two groups is that *normal people know a little quicker when their crazy ideas are crazy.*

Assisting Your Directory

Jackie is a remarkable person. Her struggles are uniquely difficult. Having recently survived the exiting of a long-term, abusive marriage, she was diagnosed with not one, but three different types of cancer. Each was successfully attacked with modern medical and surgical interventions, and she is currently in remission. She has returned to graduate school and is functioning in a very balanced but focused way. Jackie is winning.

Jackie had been a patient of mine for many months. Soon after her parents died, she had been referred by her physicians for out-patient psychotherapy. She presented as a distraught, confused, and often bewildered woman. She would take copious notes during each session. She would read and re-read an untold number of psychology-related books. I began speculating that she was changing her major from physical therapy to psychology.

During our last session together, Jackie gave me two very interesting concepts that she had garnered from our work together. One of them I'll give you in Chapter 7, but the other is appropriate to place here.

With a great sense of calmness and insight, she said, "Whenever I get overwhelmed, when I start to feel that my world is trying to make me angry and agitated, when I feel I'm about to go crazy, I just say 555-1212."

"You dial Directory Assistance?" I asked.

"Oh, no, she said.
Saying 555-1212 gives *assistance to my directory*".

"What do you mean, Jackie?"

"It has nothing to do with telephone companies. 555-1212 has to do with *Friday's Laws*. It has to do with my thalamus—my brain's directory—and my upper cerebral cortex (Appendix 1). When the Amygdala, what you called the "Chicken Little Lobe" starts screaming that my own personal sky is falling, and I get the sense that people are driving me crazy, I slowly read the 5th Law three times. I then read the 1st Law, and then the 2nd Law. Then I re- read the 1st Law and then the 2nd Law. The exercise puts me in control because I remember I am responsible for how I'm feeling and can choose how to act. It also calms me to know that life is difficult not because of my own difficulties. The whole thing takes just a couple of minutes, and it has the wondrous effect of having my upper cerebral cortex take back control from my alarm-sounding amygdala. That's how I *assist my directory*."

What a simple and effective way to apply the principles of this book. Think effectively. Know a little quicker when you have a crazy idea.

What needs to become clearer is that these Laws of Effective Thinking are interrelated *and* interdependent. They all loop and reconnect with one another. The framework that evolves is by no means a religious dictate, rather a framework that can become a refuge when life becomes chaotic. Saying 555-1212 is a way of becoming normal when you're not, staying normal when you are, and separating the two when the need arises.

Altruistic Egoism and Delayed Gratification

The building and melding of the first five Laws of Effective Thinking can lead to a more unified approach to solving problems and living well. At some point, the question arises as to what it takes to *win* in the struggling, difficult life that we all have. Taking responsibility for what we do and say, as well as our responses to what other people do and say, is an important piece of the puzzle called life. Reducing stress to realistic, manageable levels is also very important.

The late physician Dr. Hans Selye was one of the leading researchers on modern stress and stress responses. Founder of the Montreal Stress Institute and known as the "Father of Stress," Dr. Selye held that the source of human stress lies in our reactions to events, not the events themselves. He also developed the idea of *altruistic egoism* as a way of reducing stress. When combined with the behavior of *delayed gratification*, this concept offers a way of *winning* this ultimate game called life.

Altruistic egoism[6] posits that we do things for other people because of the positive way it makes us feel about ourselves when we perform these acts. Realistic good feelings about yourself are important.

Most religions of the world direct their followers to do charitable things for their fellow mankind as a way of worshiping and glorifying their particular deity or prophet. Buddhists, Christians, Muslims, Jews, and Hindus all reveal their deep faith through charitable acts. Most faiths reject any *reward* for charitable acts. The concept of *Altruistic Egoism* is meant in no way to demean or diminish charitable acts directed or based on one's faith. From a psychological perspective, however, charitable acts strongly enhance our sense of self and self-esteem. Doing things for others, knowing ahead of time that you will have an increase in positive self-esteem, is one of the requirements of effective psychological well-being. Instead of denying the good feelings that stem from charitable acts, healthy egos recognize and accept the positive aspects of doing things for other people.

Delayed gratification is the other side of the coin representing psychological health. By putting off gratification until goals are met, humans again build their self-esteem or positive egoism. This may be accomplished by not purchasing something until you have accumulated the cash to buy it; not going on vacation until there is closure on a project; or perhaps mowing the lawn before your Saturday nap in the hammock. You've probably told yourself "work before pleasure" time and again. When people set up even small rewards for accomplishing goals they feel better about themselves.

Bypass

For almost 20 years, I have volunteered to coordinate a crisis intervention program for medical technologists who operate heart-lung bypass machines during open heart surgery. Called perfusionists (they perfuse blood with oxygen after the heart is "turned off" during surgery), these technologists are under a great deal of tension and stress throughout their professional lives. Their tension is not unlike that of air-traffic controllers in that there is a great deal of repeated stress as patients *go on pump* and *come off pump*. In an effort to help these professionals balance their work responsibilities with their personal lives, my wife and I developed the following acrostic:

B Y P A S S

Balance appetites

Yield occasionally

Physical activity

Away time (daily, weekly, monthly, yearly)

Shun the *super person* urge

Schedule recreation

Some clarifications of this acrostic:

Balancing appetites has little or nothing to do with food. These appetites refer to the Greek philosopher Aristotle's concept of extreme human activities. Don't work or play too much. Avoid feast or famine. Neither play nor rest to extremes. Don't be a spendthrift, but don't hold onto your first dollar, either. In short, balance your life as much as you can.

Yielding is so very atypical-American. Imagine winning by letting go of things that, in the greater scheme of things, don't really mean very much anyway. Getting to the next red light before the kid in the car beside you. Nudging into the shortest line in the grocery store. Making sure no one else has more, bigger, or better things than you can be very, very stressful. I wonder if anyone 100 years ago pondered your struggles. I wonder if anyone 100 years from now will note the color of the next traffic light?

Physical activity and exercise are critical for effective living— not too much, not too little. Always watch out for your obsessions, denials, and avoidances.

Away time from the routines of your usual lifestyle is another way of managing stress. Take mental breaks once or twice a day. Plan to do something interesting or special every week, or at least every month or so, and look forward to it. Some very important stress modifiers are yearly breaks that can both be looked forward to and then later reflected upon (see Chapter 6).

Shun the need to always be perfect (see Chapter 7) and wonderful, especially to your children, spouse, and employees.

Scheduling of recreation needs to be done or it will never happen. Not a lot. Not too little. And never none at all. But schedule your recreation.

If you regularly implement this **BYPASS** now, you may help delay, or even eliminate, the need for bypass surgery later. *You and only you* are responsible for these aspects of your life.

I Am Responsible For Everything I Do And Say; I Am Not Responsible For Your Response

FRIDAY'S LAWS

1. Life Is Difficult.

2. Perception Is Reality.

3. Change Is The Toughest Thing A Human Being Can Do.

4. You Can Never Change Another Human Being; You Can Only Change Yourself. When You Change, They Change, But You Can Not Change Them.

5. I Am Responsible For Everything I Do And Say. I Am Not Responsible For Your Response.

6. **The Future And The Past Are Seldom As Good Or As Bad As We Anticipate Or Remember.**

7. No One Has A Squeaky Clean Psyche.

8. The Only Thing That Lasts Forever Is . . . NOW.

The Future and the Past are Seldom as Good nor as Bad as We Anticipate or Remember

There is more to life than increasing its speed.
Mahatma Gandhi

W hile in graduate school back in the early 1970s, I re-member hearing a Zen metaphor that was recently offered in Dr. Richard Carlson's [7] book, *Don't Sweat the Small Stuff.*

There was a very wise man who lived on top of a mountain in a very small country not so far away from here. In times of strife and when significant decisions had to be made, people in the surrounding villages would seek advice from this insightful elder. One day an aging farmer began the laborious three-day trek to the summit of the wise man's mountain.

"My life has been ruined," said the weary farmer to the wise man. "My only ox was just killed. My fields will never be planted and my family will starve. What should I do? This is truly the worst thing that could ever happen to a man."

The wise man turned to the farmer and replied, "Maybe so. Maybe not."

The farmer was infuriated. What a stupid answer to such a devastat-ing problem. He left in utter dismay.

On the way back to his home, the farmer came upon a wild horse that had been caught in a huge bramble bush. He captured the horse, took him home, tamed him, and was joyous. The farmer returned to the wise man to pay homage, give thanks, and to tell the wise man of his new fortune.

"Now I'll be able to plant even more crops than I could have when I had that slow, dumb ox. Truly now my family will prosper. This is the greatest thing that could happen to a poor farmer."

The wise man responded, "Maybe so. Maybe not."

Once again the old farmer was angry at the wise man. What a stupid response to such a joyous shift of fate. The farmer stormed off down the mountain with even more anger than before.

Some time later the farmer's only son, the one who did all the farm labor for his aging father, took their prized horse for a ride in the countryside. The young man was thrown from the horse and so severely broke his leg that he almost died. The farmer returned to the wise man for counsel.

"My only son, the joy of my life and the backbone of my poor working family, has fallen off the horse and broken his leg. He can do nothing. Our fields will go to furrow. Surely we will lose the little that we have and my family will starve."

The wise man looked with love at the shaken farmer and said, "Maybe so. Maybe not."

The farmer was ready to harm the wise man. Such a flip answer to the most disastrous of all possible life events. Again, the farmer stormed off in a fit of rage.

Soon this small, poor country was attacked by marauding warriors. Young men from throughout the land were conscripted into the small country's military service to defend their homeland. The small village was stripped of its youth, many of whom would surely become cannon fodder in a senseless conflict. However, the farmer's son was left at home, for his leg was too injured for him to have been of service to his country.

The future and the past are seldom as good nor as bad as we anticipate or remember.

The most common problems presented to me in therapy over the last 20 plus years have been connected to patients' concepts of future and past events. Anxiety, phobias, and depression invariably have shadows of memories and projections of fear that surround emotional symptoms. Sorting out the past and future from present functioning consumes a good deal of the energy expended in the treatment of emotional problems.

When patients present problems that indicate their failure to understand and internalize this 6th Law of Effective Thinking, I have often reflected on, and recounted, two events that happened to me.

Aunt Hilda

Several years ago I was visiting with my great-aunt Hilda Friday Weiss. She was a marvelous, warm, kind, and generous woman. Having had no children of her own, she had raised my father and Uncle J.R. when their mother died soon after giving birth. She really was more of a grandmother to me than a great-aunt.

Aunt Hilda was one of those exceptional humans who was able to live to the amazing age of 103. I would usually do my own form of a mini mental exam when we were together. Thankfully, her well-being was not compromised by either the physical or emotional problems that poor health inflicts. She certainly had a body that had borne the pressures of 10 plus decades of life, but her mind was able to fly to distant events in her childhood, and swim in the future rivers of gatherings-to-be. What a delight it was to be at her side and hear the tales of her life that began not too long after the American Civil War.

One crisp fall afternoon, shortly before her death in the Fall of 1987, I was sitting in her bedroom listening about life without telephones but with cruises on ocean liners long before the *Titanic's* maiden voyage.

"Paul, I have a problem. And I think it's in your area to solve," she said in her soft, but guttural, voice.

It's not a nice picture to imagine a seasoned therapist fretting with the anticipation of an unachievable task. Aunt Hilda had never, ever sought anything from anybody, as far as my image of her could recollect. She was the rock. She was the one with answers. I was the great-grandson who only sought sugar cookies, second helpings of Yorkshire pudding, and direct glimpses into the distant past.

"What's wrong, Aunt Hilda?"
"It's my friends," she responded.

I started the mental diagnostic discs spinning: Could she be feeling rejection, abandonment, avoidance, loneliness; reactive depression?

"What's wrong with your friends, Aunt Hilda?"

"All of my friends are in their 70s and 80s", she continued with a certain sadness in her voice. "They're so young they don't know what it is to be old." She looked up and winked at me. "Paul, remember, worrying is like a rocking chair: It gives you something to do, but it doesn't get you anywhere."

A month later, I was a pallbearer at my Aunt Hilda's funeral. That long walk down the Cathedral's center aisle, with my left hand gently resting on her draped coffin, was not as sad as I had thought it would be. The last lesson that she afforded me was the *perspectivizing* of time, and the discarding of two things: the minor daily problems that we can find so frustrating and infuriating, as well as the fixating and obsessing on things that we can't control.

I've tried to relate these two concepts to my patients who worry incessantly. With their temporal lobes, especially their amygdalas (their Chicken Little Lobes) working overtime, it becomes difficult for many people to stop the clattering admonitions and warnings of impending doom. Repeated reflection on the 6th Law shifts the emotional energy *away* from the temporal lobe and back to the upper cerebral cortex. It is the temporal lobe that is, and always will be, convinced that the *opposite* of this (as well as the other Laws of Effective Thinking), are true and correct.

*The **opposite** of the eight Laws of Effective Thinking are crazy ideas.*

Having slightly more energy in the upper cerebral cortex, so that logic and reason can be the administrators of life, is a goal of effective living. It is important, however, to keep the dictates of black-and-white values, and our irrational emotions, from hijacking Robert Hastings' train in *The Station*.

There is a test in Appendix II which you may have taken when you were reading Chapter 2. This may be a good time for you to take this test again, to see how much balance there is in your self-perception.

Gary and Lauri

Perhaps on a lighter side, an example of the 6th Law might be the story of the young man who was sitting at home one afternoon when his new girlfriend called him on the phone.

"Gary, it's Lauri.
How would you like to have dinner with me tonight?" queried the young woman.

"Sure!" he replied.
"Well, I'll have dinner with you on one condition. That you make mad, passionate love to me tonight," she said.

"Wow! What did you say?" Gary asked

"I said," repeated the young girl, "that I'll have dinner with you tonight if you take me to bed. You know that I've never done this before, and I've decided that tonight's the night, and you're the one I've selected."

The young man leaped for joy. He threw on his jacket and drove down to the nearby drugstore. He went right to the display with condoms and began perusing his choices.

The pharmacist observed the young boy walking back and forth in front of the display and knew the young man was in an obvious dilemma. "Could I help you?" the pharmacist asked.
"I think so," the young man replied. "You see, my girlfriend said we'd go out tonight, but only if I take her to bed. I've never done this before."

So the pharmacist put his arm around the lad and began a patient and thorough description of condoms and their proper usage. Gary made his choice and the pharmacist then asked how many he wanted.

"What do you mean?" asked the young man.

"Well, they come three, six, or 12 to a box."

"Oh, great!" exclaimed Gary. "Give me the family pack. I'm sure we're gonna do something all night long!"

The young lad headed home to shower and get ready. At 6:00 sharp he rang Lauri's doorbell. She gave him a big hug and invited him in to meet her parents and have dinner. As they sat down for supper, Lauri turned to Gary and asked if he would say the prayer before the meal. He said he'd be happy to, and he began to pray. And he prayed, and prayed, and prayed.

Ten minutes later he was still praying. Lauri turned to him, nudged him with her elbow, and whispered, "Gary, I didn't know you were so religious."

"Well," he replied, "I didn't know your father was a pharmacist."

The future and the past are seldom as good or as bad as we anticipate or remember

In the Introduction, I paraphrased Robert Hastings' *The Station*. For most humans, few things in life disturb the art of living and our ability to think correctly more than the "regrets over yesterday and our fears of tomorrow."

This same directive holds that if one second were two seconds long, you would be half your current age; or if one second were only half a second long, you'd be twice as old as you are now. Time is a creation of our upper cerebral cortex. Driven by logic, we have created machines that can splinter a second into billions of parts. But, astonishingly, we can never capture *now*, that one time section that we perpetually are locked into. (See Chapter 8 for a further discussion of "now.")

There is a view that holds that neither the past nor the future exists, for no one has ever been able to see five seconds, five minutes, five hours, or five years ago. Likewise no one can show you any of these time frames in the future. Neither the future nor the past exists. The description of a past event is, at best, a description of a consensus. Consensus does not dictate reality. Also the future is, at best, a probability.

Both your temporal lobe and your upper cerebral cortex register events that you have experienced. It's the temporal lobe that produces the intense emotional memories and projections that you have experienced, or thoughts of which lay ahead of you. However, it is your upper cerebral cortex that determines the probabilities and possibilities that past events have occurred. It is also the cerebral cortex that determines the probabilities and possibilities that future events will happen.

The cerebral cortex organizes whatever the temporal lobe creates or retrieves.

Ultimately, the temporal lobe is in charge of conscious and unconscious life.

When the temporal lobe makes major life decisions, the difficulties of a difficult life are increased. After all, a "foolish accident" could be just another term for an unconscious suicidal act. This is what can happen when the temporal lobe is in charge of life decisions. Examples of this constantly surround you, filling daily newspapers and television tabloid shows: Drunk-driving deaths, sexual affairs, and silly financial investments all speak to life decisions which are ultimately determined by the emotional center of our brains. When the upper cerebral cortex makes major life decisions, the difficulties of a difficult life are reduced and many would-be accidents do not occur.

The following essay was sent to me by my daughter during her freshman year at college:

Imagine there is a bank that credits your account each morning with $86,400. It carries over no balance from day to day. Every evening it deletes every part of the balance you failed to use during the day. What would you do? Draw out every cent? Of course!!

Each of us has such a bank. Its name is TIME. Every morning it credits you with 86,400 seconds. Every night it writes off, as lost, whatever of this you failed to invest to good purpose. It carries over no balance. It allows no overdraft. Each day it opens a new account for you. Each night it burns the remains of the day. If you fail to use the day's deposits, the loss is yours. There is no going back. There is no drawing against "tomorrow." You must live in the present on today's deposits. Invest it so as to get from it the utmost in health, happiness, and success.

The clock is running. Make the most of today.
Realize the value of ONE YEAR as if you were a student who failed a grade.
Realize the value of ONE MONTH as if you were a mother who gave birth to a premature baby.
Realize the value of ONE WEEK as if you were the editor of a weekly newspaper.
Realize the value of ONE HOUR as if you were the lovers who are waiting to meet.

Realize the value of ONE MINUTE as if you were a person who missed the train.

Realize the value of ONE SECOND as if you were a person who just avoided an accident.

Realize the value of ONE MILLISECOND as if you were the person who won a silver medal in the Olympics.

Treasure every moment that you have, and treasure it more because you shared it with someone special—special enough with whom to spend your time. Remember that time waits for no one. Yesterday is history. Tomorrow is a mystery. Today is a gift. That's why it's called the present .

A great deal of classic psychotherapy time has been spent reviewing past events and planning actions for the future. Yet the very nature of reflection and projection prohibits an *accurate* portrayal of past and future events. Victors write the history books. The insertion of our egos into life events changes the very events we are remembering, participating in, or planning for. As discussed in the 2nd Law (Perception Is Reality), all humans have a view of themselves and their lives, and this view is *accurate* for them. Regardless of whether you are preparing for a computer crash at the turn of the century, or reflecting on a victory or defeat in a contest in the distant past . . .

The Future And The Past Are Seldom As Good Nor As Bad As We Anticipate Or Remember

FRIDAY'S LAWS

1. Life Is Difficult.

2. Perception Is Reality.

3. Change Is The Toughest Thing A Human Being Can Do.

4. You Can Never Change Another Human Being; You Can Only Change Yourself. When You Change, They Change, But You Can Not Change Them.

5. I Am Responsible For Everything I Do And Say. I Am Not Responsible For Your Response.

6. The Future And The Past Are Seldom As Good Or As Bad As We Anticipate Or Remember.

7. **No One Has A Squeaky Clean Psyche.**

8. The Only Thing That Lasts Forever Is . . . NOW.

Nobody has a Squeaky-Clean Psyche

If parents, at least implicitly, do not give their children permission to fail, their children may succeed, but only by paying too great a price to their psychic economy. The right to fail is as inalienable as the right to equal opportunity.

—Sidney Harris

In the 1978 classic *The Road Less Traveled*, Dr. M. Scott Peck defined Original Sin as *laziness*. To me, he made a revolutionary, insightful offering. It was the melding of classic psychiatry and a formal Christian concept. Original Sin had been a religious foundation of guilt. The thought that ALL humans, even hard-working, *successful* humans, could always do more, and the idea that by doing whatever it is that we do is never enough, was an awakening. Irrational guilt began to abate. Prior to reading Dr. Peck's discourse on guilt, I had felt torn between either becoming an obsessive-compulsive, Type A, heart attack candidate or a laid-back, Type B *non-winning* loser who doesn't work or try hard enough at almost anything.

Even though few Boy Scouts will be reading this book, I suspect that most of you usually are *trustworthy, loyal, helpful, friendly, courteous, kind, obedient, cheerful, thrifty, brave, clean, and reverent* most of the time. And yet you are not perfect, and your life continues to be difficult.

Life is striving; not arriving.

Perhaps one of the unconscious, unspoken frontal lobe dictates that gets imprinted early on is that:

IF ONLY
we did a bit more homework,
tried a bit harder,
got one more degree,
earned just one million dollars more,

THEN
We would be baptized into blissful, earthly success.
We could relax and enjoy.
We would be perfect.
Life would not be difficult, but would be easy.

There would be no bills, sickness, accidents, deaths, or daily misery.

We would arrive at our own personal *Station.*
We would have formed our own squeaky-clean psyche.

Alas, it is not to be. And we will not obtain a squeaky-clean psyche by struggling and succeeding in resolving Freud's Oedipus or Electra complex. We won't get it by melding into Jung's archetypes. We won't get there by searching for Frankel's Meaning of Life, nor Carl Rodgers' fulfillment through unconditional positive regard. No matter what we do,

We will never have squeaky-clean psyches.

As described in Chapter 1, we all valiantly strive to re-experience perfection, to completely re-live those last seven months of our gestation, a period when the temporal lobe was being formed, and the foundations for the cerebral cortex were starting to develop within each of our skulls.

Our post-birth experiences are perpetually symbolized by both the innate struggle for survival, and the relationships that are forged in our socialization. Being developmental/social animals, we relate all new relationships with previous relationships. As described in the Introduction to this book, the first relationship for all humans is with our mothers in utero. As further developed in Chapter 1, the foundation for our difficult lives is the perpetual struggle to re-experience the perfection that we first encountered between the eighth and ninth week after our conception. That is the magical period when the amygdala, located deep within the temporal lobe, comes into being. Through the next seven months of our pre-birth development — during the Period of Awe — we get as close as we ever will get to perfect existence. After birth, nobody is perfect. Nobody has ever figured out how to perpetually have no wants and no needs. *Nobody has a squeaky-clean psyche.*

Your Lake

Think of yourself as a lake. The depth of the lake is equivalent to your age. If you were sitting in a boat out in the middle of this lake, how deep into the lake could you see? Given the murkiness of the average lake, you could only see perhaps a foot or two beneath the surface.

What about the water and the objects in the water below sight level? Just because you can't see them doesn't mean they don't exist. This is the metaphorical difference between our consciousness and our unconsciousness. What we can see is what we are aware of, yet this consciousness is supported by far more depth (unconsciousness) than we can ever be knowingly aware of. The clean water signifies and contains the things of which we are aware, yet this clear layer rests upon a deep, murky strata containing more life events and memories than we can ever be consciously aware of. However, all healthy lakes circulate water continuously.

Here is an exercise for you to do.

Think of a grade school teacher you had. Think of an incident you had involving this teacher. What did the classroom look like? What were you and the teacher wearing? What smells can you recall? Stop reading! Close your eyes and reflect on this exercise for a few moments.

Memory is the mental equivalent of water recirculating in a lake. The goal is not to see the bedrock or bottom of the lake. The goal of a healthy lake and psyche is to be able to circulate both water and memories freely.

Very shortly, your recollected memory of this teacher, and the incident that you've recalled, will drift back down into your unconsciousness, but this memory item, like all other significant (and many, many insignificant) memories that support your consciousness will meld into ever increasing depths of your psychological lake. Just as water that is both visible and invisible supports a boat, pleasant and bad memories are necessary to support good mental health.

Psychologists and other mental health professionals are like first mates on a captain's boat. When things go bump in the night, psychologists can don their scuba gear and check out their patient's hull beneath the water line. When he or she finds something, the therapist may want to hoist the object onto the deck for closer inspection. Breaking the disturbing object into pieces, throwing it intact up onto the shore, even putting it back into the lake, are all options that the first mate and captain (of course, the patient) can discuss. Whatever is decided, the purpose of therapeutic interventions is NOT to see the bottom of the lake - the metaphoric equivalent of having a squeaky-clean psyche. Given the constraints of human mental and spiritual capacities, the goal of therapy is to help make the womb-to-tomb trip as productive and appropriate as possible. All the therapy in the world will never make a human being's psyche squeaky-clean.

Love

Searching for *true love* is one of life's great ventures. We all strive to re-experience the perfection that we had in utero. Poets, writers, sculptors, painters, and artists from every culture since the dawn of mankind have attempted to define *love*—the most fundamental bond of all human relationships.

Psychology has defined the initial stage of love as the *limratic stage*. This is the emotionally driven sensation that most of us have experienced—and long to re-experience; that post-puberty sensation that inflames the psyches and groins of all humans. This initial stage of love is one of the few obsessive-compulsive periods (which can sometimes be so strong that it can be considered a disorder!) that society accepts without abhorrence and rejection, as long as the intensity stops within a few months, thank you very much.

This limratic stage of love is sometimes labeled *puppy love*, a demeaning term which I hold in great disdain, for I think it's grounded in the jealousy of middle or old age. We just **wish** we could re-experience our *first love*, but often feel that it is chronologically so far away from us that we can never grasp it again.

The opposite end of the love spectrum is, unfortunately, experienced by many people who have not learned to *think effectively*. Martin Seligman describes this stage of love quite well when referring to Robertson Davies' *Acedia*.

In the Middle Ages, acedia was considered one of the seven *deadly sins*. Translated as sloth or indifference, acedia eventually attacks virtually every relationship. A squeaky-clean relationship, be it in business or marriage, does not exist. We still hope and believe that, if we just hook up with that right person, that right organization or religious sect, then and only then will we be complete. Only then will we arrive at our own personal *Station*.

But I offer a psychologist's definition of love—

If external or worldly success can be defined as achieving a balance among independence, non-vulnerability, and *schmoozing*, then I see internal success as the opposite of these three qualities. Love—or internal success—is not only a willingness to be *dependent, vulnerable* and *intimate*, but love is the seeking of ways of *mutually increasing* these three qualities with the few people with whom we share a special, private, internal life. As previously described, all normally developed humans experienced mega amounts of dependency, vulnerability, and intimacy while within their mothers' wombs. This was the only time that we experienced perfection. This occurred once the amygdala was formed, at the eighth or ninth week of our gestation. Love is something that we have already experienced during the Period of Awe.

We search in the eyes and bodies of our lovers and mates for these three things in as complete a form as we can find. It never gets as good as it was before we were born, but it can, with a great deal of hard work, be approached. Dependency, Vulnerability, and Intimacy are certainly the opposite of what we cultivate, and are instructed to develop, in this post-industrial revolution/ *successful* society.

Dependent, Vulnerable, and Intimate

Just because we don't, nor does anyone else, have a squeaky-clean psyche doesn't mean that we can not *win at living*. It's not an easy thing to do. We don't *get the answer* and then sit back enjoying the rest of Hastings' trip (see Chapter 1). There is, however, a concept and guideline that can lead to a very successful life. To achieve this, you'll need to be *sociologically schizophrenic*.

In Chapter 1, the Period of Awe was described as the moment when the amygdala first come into existence and then develop for the next seven months. Because it is the only time when we are perpetually without needs or wants, it is the only time in our mortal lives when we experience perpetual perfection. It is also a time when we experience COMPLETE *dependency, vulnerability, and intimacy*. These are the components a psychologist may use to describe *love*. Love is *not* the absence of needs and wants, but the experience of *choosing* to be dependent, vulnerable, and intimate (intimacy may or may not include sexuality in its display of behaviors). This *mature love*, which has *choice* deeply incorporated in it, is different from the aforementioned limratic stage of a relationship. The limratic stage is a socially approved obsessive-compulsive disorder. A state of mind where the groins and loins drive the experience and the ventral section of the frontal lobe (where values like *should* and *shouldn't*, as well as dictates like *have to, got to,* or *must* are located) is relegated to a level of insignificance. Imagine seeking to mutually **increase** dependency on each other, searching out ways of being *more* vulnerable to slights and rejections, and seeking out ways of displaying these two attitudinal elements through intimacy by giving more than one receives.

Think back on O. Henry's wonderful story of "The Gift of the Magi."

A newly married, deeply loving, but very poor couple were caught up in the excitement of the Christmas season.

The story appears to take place in the early 1900s, when there was far less materialism and when there were deeper struggles to survive, let alone live well.

The young man and woman in O. Henry's short story each had a prized possession. She had beautiful long hair which she combed every day; he had a pocket watch which he inherited from his father, something in which he took great pride and cared for more than anything else he owned.

As the season of giving approached, and both felt a growing anxiety that they would not have something appropriate to give to their love, they made plans to make their first Christmas together a very special one.

Early Christmas morning they looked at each other softly and handed each other their small packages of love.

He opened his first and her excitement at giving this gift was far greater than what he felt when he opened it. She had bought him a watch fob, a small piece of beautifully made cloth and metal that would increase his joy at displaying his prized pocket watch. But he appeared sad as he asked his love to open her gift.

She slowly opened the brown paper sack and saw the two beautifully inscribed silver hair combs. She too became saddened. The young girl gently removed the scarf that was covering her head. She had cropped her lovely hair close to her head and sold her hair to a wig maker for the money needed to purchase her love's watch fob.

A smile crossed his face. He turned his pants pockets inside out. They were empty. He had sold his watch to get the money needed to buy the two silver hair combs—mutual dependency, vulnerability, and intimacy were in abundance.

Independent, Non-Vulnerable, and *Schmoozing*

The world outside the home and the womb is challenging. Life truly is the struggle of adaptation. Those who *win* the most in this demanding environment have learned to develop the three qualities and behaviors of independence, and non-vulnerability, plus the ability to *schmooze* well.

Independence is displayed in many ways. Having a lot of money will afford a degree of independence. Having positions of authority and power in industry incorporates a good deal of independence in your daily life. Having the ability to say "no," to be able to set your own schedules, and to come and go as you please require and grant a degree of independence.

Non-vulnerability is also displayed in effective living. People who have reasonably good health, who are able to satisfy all their needs and *most* of their wants (see Chapter 3), who have the Neurotic Delusion of Control (NDC) in reasonable balance (see Chapter 3), and who stave off attempts by others to undermine or hurt them, have degrees of non-vulnerability.

Schmoozing is an interesting Yiddish term. Loosely translated, *schmoozing* can mean the ability to be social, to be accommodating, and to relate to many different people in a pleasant, almost delightful way. However, some people believe *schmoozing* is a shallow, superficial, and manipulative behavior. If you *schmooze* well, you may be considered a nice person, perhaps a *hail fellow well met*. If done well, someone who *schmoozes* is thought to have well-developed social and interpersonal skills. If *schmoozing* is done really well, done so that no one knows it is being done and everyone feels good, it can be an art form. By effectively combining *schmoozing* with independence and non-vulnerability, one can have a very successful **external** life.

Trouble Brewing

A lot of bright, wealthy, externally successful people have had disastrous, very *unsuccessful* internal lives.

Many executives of large corporations that I've worked with professionally, along with many white and blue-collar workers whom I have seen in my office, have had well-developed, externally successful careers. Many of these same people, however, have been depressed, have been anxious, and too many of these people have had disastrous home lives.

They are estranged from their children, fight with their spouses, are angry at their parents (whether their parents are dead or alive). These externally successful people can't quite figure out how they can be so wonderfully respected by their bosses, business peers, good friends, and fellow workers, and yet be so terribly unadored by their families. They believe they are held in such low regard by those who *should* love and respect them, that they may turn to drink or drugs, spend excessive time at the club playing golf or gin rummy, and, as an interim tonic for their injured egos and souls, perhaps have a sexual tryst or affair. (See the description of the limratic stage of love above.)

Is Your Job Your Lover?

Many *successful* executives and laborers have made their jobs or occupations their lover. Their relationship with work is so special that no one else can really understand how important it truly is. Work gives these tortured, confused people a separate space, a significant time and energy investment. The process is coveted, and is seldom shared with one's spouse; time is shifted from children and family; work and home are kept away from each other. The only difference is an occasional holiday spent with the family, but this is done only occasionally.

Workaholism, alcoholism, obsessive sports, or affairs of the heart may, for a short time, renew energy or soothe the assaulted ego. The daily chores of earning a living can go on, but only for a short time. More and more time and energy are needed, and eventually, marital relationships may often pay the price for this *external success*.

There are also those people who are *overly* dependent, vulnerable, and intimate. The perfect attributes for successful *internal* living are equally disastrous when taken out of the home and into the external world and the workplace. Health care professionals who get too attached to their patients, bankers who grant too many bad loans, mental health professionals, and religious and spiritual leaders who cross the line and become physically involved with patients or members of their congregations are all examples of taking three very positive human qualities too far. These people can be *eaten alive* by the externally successful predators. So what's a person to do?

Sociological Schizophrenia

Life's true winners balance *external* and *internal* success: A kind of *sociological schizophrenia*.

They display independence, non-vulnerability, and *schmoozing* in the external world and are equally competent at displaying dependency, vulnerability, and intimacy (in-to-me-you-see?) when they cross the thresholds of their homes.

124   PAUL J. FRIDAY, Ph.D.

The Art of Successful Living lies in balancing these two opposite sets of human behaviors.

SUCCESS

EXTERNAL	*INTERNAL*
Independent	Dependent
Non-vulnerable	Vulnerable
Schmooze	Intimate

Sherri

Sherri was the most difficult, and yet most successful, patient I've had in 23 years of clinical practice. At the age of 16, she felt she knew all she needed to know, and the defiance of this red-haired, thin-lipped teenager was palpable to all who knew her, especially her parents. What she didn't know was how foolish it is to take a ride on a warm early autumn evening with two twenty-something men.

She did learn something new very quickly. Sherri was raped and left in the woods several miles from her home. She managed to crawl, walk, and finally run home. When she arrived at her doorstep at 3:30 a.m., her parents were so angry at their own fears and fantasies that they sent her directly to her room. No, she couldn't take a shower. They didn't want to hear her excuses. No, she didn't tell them, or anyone, what had happened to her on that scary, fateful night.

Twenty-seven years later, there was a knock on my door. An assertive, controlling, forceful woman asked if she could talk with me. Was I willing to take a new patient ? Sherri had a list of physical problems that kept a cadre of physicians busy for years: ulcerative colitis, irritable bowel syndrome, headaches, etc.

Psychologically, she presented a whole slew of additional problems, not the least of which were extreme anxiety and depression. Slowly we started to get to know each other. Whenever she began to sense any degree of dependency or vulnerability she would erupt in rage. She would often storm out of my office screaming that she would never come back. The slightest misinterpretation would convince her that I didn't care, that I wasn't listening, and that I was going to abandon her. It took almost three years before she let me become the first person to know what had happened to her on that fateful fall evening. The declaration of the event certainly didn't resolve her quarter century of buried issues; fears that she had fermented into a lifelong hatred and distrust of two categories of people: men and herself. Certainly anyone who cared for her must either be inherently deceitful and dangerous, or foolish and stupid.

Sherri was in therapy with me for almost eight years. She represented a Managed Care company's nightmare, a therapist's ultimate challenge, and a potential reward for helping her to overcome the struggle of her life. With each blocking situation that arose, or that she created, she learned that dependency, vulnerability, and intimacy were not only post-traumatically possible, but were able to be successfully balanced with independence, non-vulnerability, and *schmoozing*.

Sociological schizophrenia needs to be decided upon in a well-reasoned, safe environment. A decision to balance internal and external success is not made lightly, nor just once. The framework for this decision is the Eight Laws of Thinking Effectively. In Sherri's case, this framework was consistently reviewed, but these Laws were not the reason, nor the catalyst, for her successful changes. The crucible that her recovery was formed in is euphemistically called the therapeutic process, a change that is described at length in the Epilogue. This change, however, does not, and never was meant to lead to a perfect state of mind, for . . .

No One Has A Squeaky-Clean Psyche.

FRIDAY'S LAWS

1. Life Is Difficult.

2. Perception Is Reality.

3. Change Is The Toughest Thing A Human Being Can Do.

4. You Can Never Change Another Human Being; You Can Only Change Yourself. When You Change, They Change, But You Can Not Change Them.

5. I Am Responsible For Everything I Do And Say. I Am Not Responsible For Your Response.

6. The Future And The Past Are Seldom As Good Or As Bad As We Anticipate Or Remember.

7. No One Has A Squeaky Clean Psyche.

8. **The Only Thing That Lasts Forever Is . . . NOW.**

8

THE ONLY THING THAT LASTS FOREVER
IS ... NOW

Tom Seaver, a former pitcher for the New York Mets, reportedly asked his manager, the great sage Yogi Berra, "Hey, Yogi, what time is it?" Berra answered:
"You mean now?"

What is time? The shadow on the dial, the striking of the clock, the running of the sand through the hour glass, day and night, summer and winter, month, years, centuries—these are but the arbitrary and outward signs, the measures of Time itself. Time is the Life of the soul.

Henry Wadsworth Longfellow

*The time on either side of **now** stands fast.*

Maxine Kumin

T he post-industrialized world has become obsessed with time. This has insidiously forced us to live in the past and future, time zones created by the logic of the upper cerebral cortex. We often wallow through and perpetually fight in the sphere that Hastings labeled *regrets over yesterday and fears of tomorrow. Twin thieves that rob us of today.*

When people begin to wrestle with this, the last of *Friday's Laws*, they begin to tie together all the concepts of Effective Thinking.

Invariably there is an initial rejection of the *idealism* of this 8th Law. There usually is disdain with the perspectivizing of the cornerstones of planning and remembering.

When planning and remembering are seen as activities in the "now," there is a growing sense of awareness of what this whole *change business* is all about.

I recall asking a particularly troubled lawyer several years ago, "show me five minutes from now. Show me five minutes ago." He was initially confused, for he had billed his clients in time increments for so long that he couldn't fathom time's non-existence.

Outside of human perception, neither five minutes ago nor five minutes from now exists. The upper cerebral cortex is able to perspectivize time as can the two brain sections, the frontal and temporal lobes, where these two time frames are projected. The upper cerebral cortex is the section of the brain that comprehends the frontal and temporal lobes. However, the frontal and temporal lobes cannot comprehend the other part of the cerebral cortex. And yet the frontal and temporal lobes perpetually swirl in the regrets of yesterday and fears of tomorrow. Not so for the upper cerebral cortex! It understands that **now** is the only thing that lasts forever.

Several years ago, a patient of mine, Frank, who had aerophobia (a fear of airplanes and flight), was returning from a lecture series in Southern California when, at 35,000 feet above the earth, he began to ponder his death. The day before, a door had blown off an airplane shortly after taking off from Hawaii. A passenger had been sucked out of the airplane, never to be found again. Approaching the spectacular view of the Grand Canyon, and sitting next to an emergency exit, he wondered what would happen were he to be suddenly pushed into the nothingness of space.

"If I died *before* I exited the plane, then there would be nothing to worry about. If I survived the exit, I would be alive *now*," he said.

After mentally falling to within four miles from the earth, Frank related the continuing fantasy that he would be still alive. "If not, there would be nothing to worry about." Frank's mental monologue continued for several minutes. "At three, two, and one miles from impact, either I would be alive or I would not."

I pondered the restructuring and resolution of his problem. Frank was implementing the 8th Law. Even when he *pushed the envelope* by *transcending the absurd* to surviving the drop into the extra mile of the Grand Canyon's depth, he understood the need to live in the *now*. Frank said, as he left our therapy session, "*Either you are alive, or you aren't.* He then added, After all, Doc, *life is a terminal disease—sexually transmitted and incurable.*

In one of our final sessions, Frank declared that the craziest, most impossible sentence he had ever heard consisted of only three words: "I am dead."

For the next several months, I queried many of my patients (many of my most profound ideas have stemmed from my intimate dialogues with these marvelous people) about what they thought lasted forever. Love was soon rejected. Ideas, wealth, fame, and even families soon followed. My strongly spiritual patients have offered that God, the soul, and spirits last forever.

However, because these patients were not consciously cognizant of **anything** either **before** the formation of their amygdala nor **after** our last exhalation, these were consigned to the huge area of strong beliefs.

The *goal of effective thinking* is **not** to have either the temporal or frontal lobe become the logical, reasonable sections of the upper cerebral cortex. The object of Effective Thinking is to have the higher order of logic and reason obtain the necessary insight to provide direction for humans to survive. To think effectively and win the daily struggles of living, we must recognize our *crazy ideas* a little quicker. Neither the frontal nor temporal lobes *dictate* behavior when we accept that . . .

The Only Thing That Lasts Forever Is . . . NOW.

Epilogue

How Does Psychotherapy Work?

Oh, the comfort, the inexpressible comfort of feeling safe with a person Having neither to weigh thoughts , nor measure words; but pouring them all right out just as they are chaff and grain together; certain that a faithful hand will take and sift them; keep what is worth keeping, and then with a breath of kindness, blow the rest away.

Dinah Marie Mulock Craik, (from *A Life for a Life*)

Words change the structure of the human brain. This is the *how* and *why* of successful psychotherapy. The brain changes when it is exposed to the right words in the right way. Modern technology in the form of SPECT and PET[8] scanners has been able to document the structural changes that occur when human brains are exposed to just the right sequence of words. For example, patients placed in a PET scanner who are severely depressed have their *right* ventral area of their frontal lobes show up as "hot" (red or orange). When these patients feel less depressed, the *left* ventral area of their frontal lobe becomes red or orange. Research on "false memory" has been fascinating. We know that the process of storing and consolidating new memories into permanent storage can take months, if not years. However, this process of memory creation can be disrupted by head injuries and ECT (electro-convulsive shock therapy). Once permanently stored, memories can still be influenced by subsequent experiences, like hypnosis. Thus previously held beliefs can be altered through certain encounters, like being in a cult or involved in psychotherapy. Obviously these changes can be positive or negative depending on perceptions and values. How these changes specifically occur are still unknown.

In therapy, words and the process of therapy help to resolve emotional problems and promote healing. In life, many words heal, and many words harm.

Imagine that you are sitting at home when the phone rings:

"Mrs. Jones? My name is Officer Thomas Moore from the Sacramento police department. I'm sorry to inform you that your son has been involved in a car accident and has been fatally injured."

The physical reactions to these words are common: narrowing of visual fields, shortness of breath, an inability to speak. The memory of that moment and those words would be literally etched deep inside the brain, recalled and relived forever. But think about this. The above three sentences incorporate 33 English words. Words. Words change the structure of the human brain.

A short time later, the phone rings again:
"Mrs. Jones? This is Officer Frank Semper. I'm terribly sorry, but Officer Moore called the wrong Mrs. Jones. Your son was not the person involved in the accident this afternoon. Your son is perfectly all right."

Five sentences, 36 words. Words. Words change the structure of the human brain.

As I stated in the Introduction to this book, the Eight Laws of Thinking Effectively describe the human condition when the brain sections work well together. *Friday's Laws* contain 86 words. They can change the structure of your brain.

Friday's Laws are similar to Newton's Laws of Physics in that they describe human beings when they are thinking effectively. One of the Newtonian Laws of Physics describes all objects, regardless of mass, falling at 32 feet per second squared. There are no values and no emotions in either of these two systems of laws. However, values and emotions are imposed upon every human being who has ever lived—just as emotions are imposed upon us when a loved one perishes in a horrendous airplane crash—a crash caused by or responding to a law of physics

Friday's Laws, when taken as a whole, will help soothe the psyche, if not the soul. However, *cures* for serious emotional problems come from the *therapeutic process,* not from a set of Laws of Effective Thinking. *Process* is psychotherapy's most important product.

The Therapeutic Process

The therapeutic process, the byproduct of tremendous efforts and energy on the parts of both therapists and patients, can generate emotional and psychological healing. The process calls for an *absence* of mutual independence, an *absence* of mutual non-vulnerability, and an ability to cut through the *schmoozing.*

Successful psychotherapy ferrets out therapeutic dependency, vulnerability, and intimacy. These are the same components that a child senses in utero with its Maker during the Period of Awe. In the last seven months of our gestation, the upper cerebral cortex and frontal lobe are in their developmental infancy, while the temporal lobe is in the Period of Awe. Dependency, vulnerability, and intimacy are the same components that make a good relationship or marriage. It is these same components that are strongly interwoven in effective psychotherapy, but without the potential for sexual intimacy between therapist and patient.

I have worked with thousands of patients, each one of whom has offered me some insight into the human condition. I surely have learned as much from my patients as they have gained from the hours spent in search of resolutions for their psychological maladies. I can assure you that if change has occurred, and I believe substantial changes do occur in psychotherapy, it is NOT the result of memorizing a list of 86 words in *Friday's Laws*. Nor does change occur through the use of drug therapy. The therapeutic process is not simple; it can get very confusing. When done correctly, however, it is seldom wrong.

The Therapeutic Process: How Does it Work?

When two people learn how to suspend the judgmental and logical thinking processes, and trust the deeper temporal lobe-driven connectedness that is learned in the womb, *then* this process can take place. The therapeutic process, like emotions, is neither logical nor necessarily reasonable. This is the major connecting problem between classical Western medical practices and the processes found in effective relationships. The upper cerebral cortex has been *the* driving force in Western medicine. Logic and reason are the palace guards; logic and reason don't *trust* values and emotions. The handmaidens of medicine, the touching and holding of the patient's fears, are relegated to the *lower areas* of the frontal and temporal lobes. Emotions and values don't *trust* logic and reason. Logic and reason have no instincts for what is truly important in life. Many smart doctors are inadequate physicians. Many excellent psychotherapists are not very intelligent. When thoughts, values, and emotions are mutually supportive, life's experiences become as interesting, pleasurable, and effective as they can be. Balance, as espoused as far back as the ancient Greeks, is the Holy Grail of effective living.

The *theoretically ideal* human might have a mental-energy-distribution between the upper cerebral cortex, frontal lobe, and temporal lobe of 34%, 33% and 33% respectively. Why this division? If logic and reason are *slightly* more influential on behavior than values and emotions, the probability arises that reasonable life choices are going to be made. When the upper cerebral cortex, not the frontal nor temporal lobe, is the administrator of your life, you can approach this theoretically ideal balance. Notice that *slightly more influence* is not a *domination* by logic and reason. Logic dominating would be no healthier than having values or emotions dominate the daily activities of life.

The other end of the mental-energy distribution spectrum, having emotions and values slightly to extremely more powerful than logic and reasoning, is also a sign of living less than ideally. Balance is the goal. Regardless of the area of domination, people who are grossly out of balance tend to be very difficult to be around or to live with.

When humans experience the similar connectedness that was first sensed in the last seven months of our gestation, the therapeutic process can evoke significant changes in humans. This *inside success* (Chapters 1 and 7) is difficult to accomplish once we are born; it certainly doesn't occur as often as professionals and their financial supporters (insurance companies) wish it would, *but* it does happen, and when it does, it is difficult to measure, let alone understand.

Mentoring

When there is communication on a therapeutic level, the individuals involved feel something very deeply. It is a very special temporal-lobe-driven experience. Mentoring, as well as effective psychotherapy, encompasses this level of communication.

People who have not experienced this level of trust, who have not been with others with the deep emotions of the temporal lobe, will tend to ridicule and reject the process. These people will try to force *science* to explain what the temporal lobe already knows, and the upper cerebral cortex doesn't know and can never comprehend. There is something fascinating about the rejection, though. The stronger the rejection of this process, the stronger the yearning is to be able to experience it.

There is a level of touching and being with someone that the upper cerebral cortex cannot comprehend, cannot understand, cannot describe in words. There are no language receptor sites in the temporal lobe, so there can't be any *dialogue* (in a language sense) between these two sections of the human brain. This lack of *language knowledge* is what is so frustrating to a physician who *knows* the didactic process thoroughly, and science deeply, but hasn't learned to touch the patient. Often, for unknown or idiopathic reasons, many of these patients do not heal.

There are nurses who complete all the paperwork necessary for regulatory approval, but who have never given a patient a back rub. These nurses can't understand why the patient isn't appreciative of their efforts. The same dilemma is found with lawyers who know the letter of the law but don't care about justice, or the business people who downsize companies and are not aware of the devastation that is experienced at losing a 30-year job.

These professionals will scoff at the concept of the therapeutic process, for they find *sociological schizophrenia* (Chapter 7) an abhorrent concept. Or, worse, they will advocate the balancing of inside and outside living without comprehension of what it takes to accomplish its rewards.

As a student at the University of Vienna in the mid-1960s, I perused the writings of an Austrian-born English philosopher named Ludwig Wittgenstein. Mr. Edward Mowatt was my guide on this sojourn. Wittgenstein's professional goal was to write a mathematically based philosophy that was so logical and perfect that no other philosophical work would need to be written. Called the *Tractatus Logico Philosophicus* (or the *Tractatus*), this work would be so precise, so upper cerebral-cortex-driven, that no additional philosophical work would need to be created. (Ludwig Wittgenstein obviously did not understand the 7th Law.) But, as a 19 or 20 year old, I found the concept of perfection enticing. In spite of questioning Wittgensteinian perfection, I have, nonetheless, been fascinated by the final sentence to his life's major work:

Wovon man nicht sprechen kann, darüber muss man schweigen.
(What we cannot speak about, must be consigned to silence.)

What Ludwig Witgenstein did not understand though, is that the Temporal Lobe is *never* silent.

Amygdala

The amygdala is the emotional sentinel of the brain (Greek for *almond*). It is an oval or almond-sized clump of neuronal masses that is one cubic centimeter in approximate size and 600 milligrams in weight. One *amygdala* is situated on either side of the *thalamus*, near the top of the *upper brain stem*. It is a dense nugget of nerve fibers located deep inside the *temporal lobe* and is the site of powerful response emotions like fight/flight. It fires off directives for survival long before the *upper cerebral cortex* is cognizant of the perception of threat. Some consider the *amygdala* the soul of the human brain. It holds the most basic of the higher order survival functions of human beings. It continually sends out either a steady all-clear or an alarm signal to the rest of the brain.

Brain Stem

A stalk-like structure that connects the *cerebrum* with the *spinal cord*. The *brain stem*, the Ancient Reptilian Brain, evolved between 100 and 300 million years ago, and is similar to a reptilian brain. The bottom part of the brain stem controls breathing, heartbeat, and many other body processes. The major sensory and motor pathways between the body and the *cerebrum* pass through the *brain stem*.

Cerebral Cortex

A thin, but multi-folded layer of nerve cell bodies which forms the outermost part of the *cerebrum*. The *cerebral cortex* and *cerebrum* of the Modern Mammalian Brain evolved 30-40 million years ago, and are the location of modern man's language and logic centers. Together they make up 85% of the 3-pound adult brain (which is one pound at birth.) The *cerebral cortex* folds in upon itself and so forms a surface with many ridges and grooves. This folding greatly increases the surface area of the *cortex* within the limited space of the skull. The *upper cerebral cortex* objectively determines the probabilities and possibilities of successful behaviors. The cerebral cortex is considered to include four areas: The frontal, temporal, parietal and occipital lobes or sections.

Cerebrum

The large round brain structure that is divided into two *cerebral hemispheres* by a deep median sagittal groove, and joined at the bottom by the *corpus callosum*. Combined with the covering of the *cerebral cortex*, the *cerebrum* comprises the major part of the human brain. Each hemisphere is divided into four sections or lobes, each of which is named by the bone that sits on top of it: the *frontal, temporal, occipital,* and *parietal lobes.*

Frontal Lobe

The front most of the four lobes of the cerebrum and the youngest section of the modern human brain. The frontal lobe, where values are stored, evolved about 50,000 years ago. 15,000 years later, the Neanderthals (who had flat foreheads and therefore no space to house a frontal lobe) vanished from the Earth. The frontal lobe monitors our social interactions and controls the expression of our values. The frontal lobe is also the site of abstract thinking, planning, and language.

Hippocampus

Also known as the olfactory brain, the *hippocampus*, the *senses-to memory transformer,* is a sea-horse shaped structure that separates and then wraps around the *thalamus* which itself is divided into two sections. The two *amygdala*, one on each side of the divided thalamus, sit at the bottom tip of the divided hippocampus. It is an important part of the *limbic system* and is involved in some aspects of memory, in the control of autonomic functions, and in emotional expression. New events are encoded into long-term memories in the hippocampus. It is a temporary buffer zone in which this encoding takes place. The memories themselves are stored throughout the cerebral cortex.

Hypothalamus

A complex brain structure composed of many nuclei with various functions including housekeeping functions and hormonal regulation. ("Hypo" means lower and it is located below the thalamus.) It is the head ganglion of the autonomic nervous system and is involved in the control of many things, including heat regulation, heart rate, blood pressure, respiration, and sexual activity. Water, fat, and carbohydrate metabolism, as well as digestion, appetite, and body weight, are also regulated by this small structure that sits snugly against the upper brain stem. The hypothalamus also controls the activity of the nearby pituitary gland, the master gland of the body.

Limbic System

Known as the visceral brain, the limbic system is a group of brain structures that include the amygdala, hippocampus, and other closely interconnected, deep brain sections involved in emotional responses, memory formation, and movement.

Temporal Lobe

The temporal lobe of the Ancient Mammalian Brain evolved 130 million years ago. It is located at the lower side of the cerebral cortex and is the home of the amygdala. It functions in speech, as well as in auditory and complex visual perceptions.

Thalamus

The thalamus consists of two egg-shaped masses of nerve tissue. It acts like *directory assistance* or a computer modem for filtering and directing sensory information from the body to the *cerebral cortex* and back again. It may also play a part in short- and long-term memory.

Appendix II

B B T
"Balanced Brain Test"

Created By: PAUL J. FRIDAY, PH.D.

This is a test of how you see yourself NOW. It will be as accurate as you are honest. The results are not cast in stone. If you took this test before you read the book, you may want to take it again when you are finished with the book. The differences may be very interesting.

If perception is reality, then how we perceive ourselves is *realistic*. Is this an accurate view? Is it *reality*?

Imagine your boss, your sibling, child, co-worker, parent, lover, or spouse filling out the test with their perceptions of you. Would the scores be the same ? If they were different, would they be "wrong" ? Perhaps an average or consensus score would be the most accurate portrayal of you. What about your scores on this test in a week or a year? Will they be the same? If the scores are different, would that make these scores wrong?

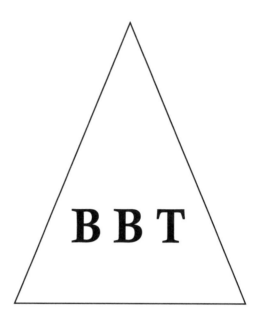

BALANCED BRAIN TEST

Over the years, psychologists have classified behaviors in many ways, such as *introvert* or *extrovert, passive* or *aggressive,* etc. Another way to view ourselves is to look at how in-balance or out-of-balance our brain function is.

This test will show you the relative strengths and influences between several sections of your brain. While you are taking this test, concentrate on your actual daily behaviors, not your intended behaviors

BEHAVIOR, NOT INTENTION
IS WHAT IS IMPORTANT!

INSTRUCTIONS

From this list of words select those that describe you, or which you feel most apply to your everyday behavior. **HOWEVER** you may only choose **15** – no more, and no less – from the list. You may want to use a pencil in order to erase before making your final selections. Study the list carefully and be ruthlessly honest. CIRCLE THE **15** NUMBERS NEXT TO EACH WORD THAT BEST DESCRIBES YOU **NOW.** Remember, BEHAVIOR, not IN-TENTION is what is important !

1. sympathetic	16. judgmental	31. helpful
2. expressive	17. procrastinating	32. rebellious
3. aware/alert	18. intelligent	33. responsible
4. protective	19. opinionated	34. giving
5. affectionate	20. sensuous	35. shy
6. reasonable	21. decisive	36. methodical
7. moralizing	22. rigid	37. inspiring
8. complying	23. curious	38. yielding
9. evaluative	24. realistic	39. sensible
10. nurturing	25. critical	40. right (correct)
11. withdrawing	26. clinging	41. imaginative
12. autonomous	27. rational	42. concise
13. encouraging	28. soothing	43. demanding
14. impulsive	29. spontaneous	44. uninhibited
15. organized	30. objective	45. unemotional

SCORE SHEET
Circle the numbers that correspond to your selected words. Circle ONLY
15 numbers

1	2	3
4	5	6
7	8	9
10	11	12
13	14	15
16	17	18
19	20	21
22	23	24
25	26	27
28	29	30
31	32	33
34	35	36
37	38	39
40	41	42
43	44	45
_____ Total	_____ Total	_____ Total
FL	TL	UCC

TOTAL: Count the number of circles in each column;
         Place that number at the bottom of each column

         Do the three numbers at the bottom of the three
         columns add up to 15?

Move those scores to the appropriate space on the brain diagram.

FL=Frontal Lobe

TL=Temporal Lobe

UCC=Upper Cerebral Cortex

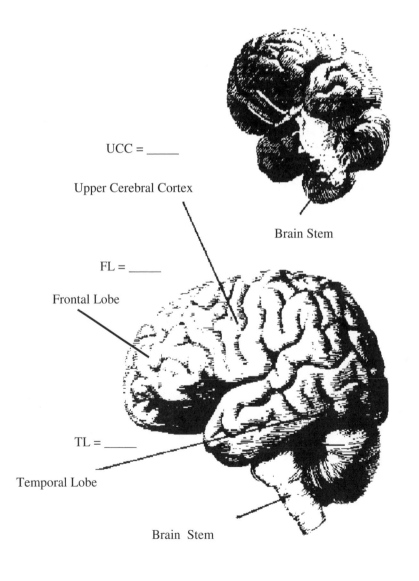

UCC = _____

Upper Cerebral Cortex

Brain Stem

FL = _____

Frontal Lobe

TL = _____

Temporal Lobe

Brain Stem

INTERPRETATION:

A goal of effective living is to have balance in your life. Don't eat too little or too much; don't spend everything you have and don't pinch every penny you earn; don't be obsessive about exercise and don't sit around doing nothing. The list could go on and on.

Balance can also be seen as an appropriate way to think, feel and display values. The test that you have just taken gives you a picture of you as you see yourself, at this point in your life. Your score indicates how balanced you are from the perspective of thinking (upper cerebral cortex functioning), your base emotions (temporal lobe functioning) and your values (frontal lobe functioning). A goal may be to have your scores fall between a 4 and 6 in each of these three categories. The avoidance of extremes is an excellent way of controlling stress.

Of course there are times in the day as well as periods in our life when a higher score in one area is appropriate. For example, there are times when we should be religious or judgmental (frontal lobe control), there are times to fight or flight problems (temporal lobe control) and there are times to calculate or fix things (cerebral cortex control.)

Ideally, though, it is the cerebral cortex that makes the decision on which section is to dominate, not the frontal nor temporal lobe.

Is there such a thing as a *perfect score* on the BBT ? Perhaps a 6 in the cerebral cortex and a 5 and a 4 in one of the other two sections.

But who has a squeaky-clean psyche?

Reference

1. Diagrams and discussion of brain locations can be found in Appendix I.

2. Amygdala—a term used in anatomical nomenclature to designate the densely packed almond-shaped bundle of neurons located deep within the temporal lobe of the brain at the tip of the hippocampal horn. See Appendix I for a graphic depiction of the location of the amygdala.

3. Reported "near death experiences" often incorporate a "blinding white light." It is possible that this is the simple retrieval of our earliest post-birth experience that was etched into our cerebral memory banks at the moment of our birth.

4. See Chapter 1 for a description of the Period of Awe and a Table to calculate yours. Also see the definition of *Love* in Chapter 7.

5. After graduating from the University of Pittsburgh in the 1980s, Danny Marino catapulted into the National Football League. By the mid 1990s he was considered one of the preeminent quarterbacks in the NFL.

6. Note that *egoism* is not *egotisticalism. Egoism* refers to how we regard ourselves and is not to be confused with egotisticalism, which is undue pride or an inflated sense of self.

7. Richard Carlson, Ph.D., Hyperion, 114 Fifth avenue, New York, NY 10011

8. PET (Positron Emission Tomography) along with SPECT (Single Photon Emission Computed Tomography) have expanded the horizons of nuclear medicine with their unique diagnostic capabilities for imaging metabolic body function.

Suggested Reading

James M, Jongeward D. Born To Win: Transactional Analysis with Gestalt Experiments. Addison-Wesley Publishing Company. Reading, MA

Jastrow R. The Enchanted Loom. Simon and Schuster Publishing, New York, NY

Peck MS. The Road Less Traveled. A New Psychology of Love, Traditional Values and Spiritual Growth. Simon and Schuster Publishing, New York, NY

Peck MS. Further Along The Road Less Traveled. The Unending Journey Toward Spiritual Growth. Simon and Schuster, New York, NY.

Carlson R. Don't Sweat the Small Stuff—and It's All Small Stuff. Hyperion Press, New York, NY

Covey SR. The Seven Habits of Highly Effective People. Restoring the Character Ethic. Simon and Schuster, New York, NY

Nuland SB. How We Die. Reflections on Life's Final Chapter. Alfred A. Knopf, Inc. New York, NY

LeDoux J. The Emotional Brain. Simon & Schuster, New York, NY

Rogers CR. A Way of Being. Houghton Mifflin Company, Boston, MA

Wittgenstein L. *Tractatus Logico-Philosophicus*. Routledge & Kegan Paul, London, England. The Humanities Press, New York, NY

Frankl VE. Man's Search For Meaning. An Introduction to Logotherapy. Touchstone Book. Simon & Schuster, New York, NY

Acknowledgments

My strongest and most sincere acknowledgment is directed to my patients. For over 20 years, each and every one of them has helped me grow some way in the understanding and love of the human spirit. The strongest and wisest people that I have known have walked through my office door or let me enter their hospital rooms. Their patience and courage in letting me see their worlds through their eyes and psyches is the ultimate stuff of *Friday's Laws*.

My father, mother, and three siblings created the bedrock of my physical and social being. Dad's quest for learning through the written word; Mom's drive to succeed and survive come whatever; my older brother Rick, with his intelligence and force, as well as my younger sister Betsy's desire for love and understanding, and my younger brother Peter's ability to pull all of it together, made a stage from which I observed life's evolution. From this springboard came my basic questioning of self and others. I learned what it took to survive in this world of mine.

Stephen Albert, Barbara and Paul Wachter, Dr. Carl Srodes, Louis Borelli, Mary Alice and Richard Gorman, Gary Matassa, and my older brother's wife, Dr. Patricia Friday, selfishly donated their valuable time to read, and then re-read again and again, excerpts of *Friday's Laws*. Each one of these friends, colleagues, and family members had his or her own way of pushing me further into creating this work. They each provided pieces of the *normal puzzle,* teaching me what it takes to help people become normal when they're not and how to help people to stay normal when they are. The editors provided both technical advice and direction. They taught me that how I speak, and how I listen, have little to do with how to put ideas onto paper. I hope these lessons hold. Eugene Kail has been a lifelong friend and consummate guardian of the English language. Eugene taught with me during the 1970s, stood with me at my wedding, and finally helped guide me at the end stage of this creation. I will always be indebted.

Many professional colleagues, such as Drs. Joseph Utley, Dennis Meisner, and W. Gerald Rainer, afforded me lecture forums where the concepts embodied in this work were formulated. Also, many organizations such as the American Society of Extra-Corporeal Technology, the American Association of Nephrology Nurses, the American Society of Travel Agents, The Colorado Medical Society, and the American Society of Radiological Technology, invited me to participate in conferences throughout the United States, Canada, and Europe. The participants at these and many other meetings provided input to help forge, mold, and flesh out the details of this work. I will always be grateful for their support and encouragement.

Drs. Daniel Sheahan, William Hawthorne, David Servan-Schreiber, Rob Fields, and Lewis Mehl-Madrona massaged the technical, neuroanatomy sections of this book. Mark Patts' patience and creative juices in designing the cover and support layouts for *Friday's Laws* were professional and timely. Walter Srokie's artistic contributions helped make this work special.

My early memories, which are always the foundation of any piece of literature or art, were tempered by the love and guidance of Anna Burt. Anna lived with our family from the time I was born until I was in high school. From teaching me to tie the laces of my first PF Flyers to sitting at the breakfast table with reading primers, Anna was the strongest of my early supports. My family experiences were combined with the shaping and imprinting of neighbors and extended family like Robert and Lou Brown, Charles and Martha Vogt, and Walter and Mae Stern. Through all of these influences, I began to be and have evolved into who I am.

My sincere gratitude to Bradley Oak Publications, their many support personnel, and Rosann Bost, the senior managing editor. Together they provided an unfailing commitment and belief in my work. I'm sure I would still be searching and roaming those lonely, painful canyons of New York rejection without their encouragement.

There are many other friends and family members who have helped in this endeavor, and while too many to mention, I will always be in their debt.

I have an extraordinary support system in my wife and daughters. My wife Patricia, my life companion, and my daughters, Alison and Erika, were always there when I needed them. They patiently tolerated my 10-hour work days and the hundreds of seminars and lectures that consumed the professional part of my existence. They are my true soulmates on my womb-to-tomb trip.

Paul J. Friday, Ph.D.
April 1999

NOTES

NOTES

NOTES

NOTES

NOTES

ORDER TODAY

BRADLEY OAK PUBLICATIONS
PO BOX 111595
1310 OLD FREEPORT ROAD,
PITTSBURGH, PENNSYLVANIA 15238
USA
1(800) 379-3180

FRIDAY'S LAWS

How to Become Normal When You're Not And How To Stay Normal When You Are

NAME ⎯⎯⎯⎯⎯⎯⎯⎯⎯⎯⎯⎯⎯⎯⎯⎯⎯⎯⎯⎯⎯⎯

ADDRESS ⎯⎯⎯⎯⎯⎯⎯⎯⎯⎯⎯⎯⎯⎯⎯⎯⎯⎯⎯⎯

CITY ⎯⎯⎯⎯⎯⎯⎯⎯⎯⎯⎯ STATE ⎯⎯⎯⎯ ZIP ⎯⎯⎯⎯

ORDER TODAY

BRADLEY OAK PUBLICATIONS
PO BOX 111595
1310 OLD FREEPORT ROAD,
PITTSBURGH, PENNSYLVANIA 15238
USA
1(800) 379-3180

FRIDAY'S LAWS

How to Become Normal When You're Not And How To Stay Normal When You Are

NAME ⎯⎯⎯⎯⎯⎯⎯⎯⎯⎯⎯⎯⎯⎯⎯⎯⎯⎯⎯⎯⎯⎯

ADDRESS ⎯⎯⎯⎯⎯⎯⎯⎯⎯⎯⎯⎯⎯⎯⎯⎯⎯⎯⎯⎯

CITY ⎯⎯⎯⎯⎯⎯⎯⎯⎯⎯⎯ STATE ⎯⎯⎯⎯ ZIP ⎯⎯⎯⎯

_____ COPY (IES)* @ $21.95 EA. (US) $ _____

PA RESIDENTS ADD APPROPRIATE SALES TAX

SHIPPING & HANDLING   **4.50**

TOTAL (CHECK OR MONEY ORDER) $ _____

CHECKS MADE PAYABLE TO - - **BRADLEY OAK PUBLICATIONS**

GIVE THE GIFT OF *EFFECTING THINKING*

*QUANTITY DISCOUNTS AVAILABLE ON ORDERS OF 10 OR MORE

Visit our web site - - fridayslaws.com

_____ COPY (IES)* @ $21.95 EA. (US) $ _____

PA RESIDENTS ADD APPROPRIATE SALES TAX

SHIPPING & HANDLING   **4.50**

TOTAL (CHECK OR MONEY ORDER) $ _____

CHECKS MADE PAYABLE TO - - **BRADLEY OAK PUBLICATIONS**

GIVE THE GIFT OF *EFFECTING THINKING*

*QUANTITY DISCOUNTS AVAILABLE ON ORDERS OF 10 OR MORE

Visit our web site - - fridayslaws.com

FRIDAY'S LAWS©

1. Life is difficult.
2. Perception is reality.
3. Change is the toughest thing a human being can do.
4. You can not change another human being, you can only change yourself.
    Once you change, they change, but you can not change them.
5. I am responsible for everything I do and say.
    I am not responsible for your response.
6. The future and the past are seldom as good or as bad as we anticipate or remember.
7. No one has a squeaky-clean psyche.
8. The only thing that lasts forever is . . . *now*

FRIDAY'S LAWS ©

1. Life is difficult.
2. Perception is reality.
3. Change is the toughest thing a human being can do.
4. You can not change another human being, you can only change yourself.
    Once you change, they change, but you cannot change them.
5. I am responsible for everything I do and say. I am not responsible for your response.
6. The future and the past are seldom as good or as bad as we anticipate or remember.
7. No one has a squeaky-clean psyche.
8. The only thing that lasts forever is . . . *Now.*

FRIDAY'S LAWS ©

1. Life is difficult.
2. Perception is reality.
3. Change is the toughest thing a human being can do.
4. You can not change another human being, you can only change yourself.
    Once you change, they change, but you cannot change them.
5. I am responsible for everything I do and say. I am not responsible for your response.
6. The future and the past are seldom as good or as bad as we anticipate or remember.
7. No one has a squeaky-clean psyche.
8. The only thing that lasts forever is . . . *Now.*

FRIDAY'S LAWS©

How To Become Normal When You're Not
And
How To Stay Normal When You Are

A book by Paul J. Friday, Ph.D.

Now Available Through   **Bradley Oak Publications**
P.O. Box 111595
1310 Old Freeport Road
Pittsburgh, PA 15238
1 – 800 – 379 – 3180

You can visit us at our web site - fridayslaws.com

FRIDAY'S LAWS ©
How To Become Normal
When You're Not
And
How To Stay Normal When
You Are
A book by Paul J. Friday, Ph.D.

Now Available Through

Bradley Oak Publications
P.O. Box 111595
1310 Old Freeport Road
Pittsburgh, PA 15238
1 – 800 – 379 – 3180

You can visit us at our web
site
fridayslaws.com

FRIDAY'S LAWS ©
How To Become Normal
When You're Not
And
How To Stay Normal When
You Are
A book by Paul J. Friday, Ph.D.

Now Available Through

Bradley Oak Publications
P.O. Box 111595
1310 Old Freeport Road
Pittsburgh, PA 15238
1 – 800 – 379 – 3180

You can visit us at our web
site
fridayslaws.com